The Residue of Marriage & Divorce

The issues no one wants to talk about

www.rcwiconsultants.com

ISBN-13:
978-1495983818

ISBN-10:
1495983811

No part of this book may be reproduced or transmitted in any form or by any mean, electronic or mechanical – including photocopying, recording, or by any information storage and retrieval systems – without permission via email from the author. Please direct all inquiries to theresidueofmarriageanddivorce@gmail.com

Victoria,   12/5/14

Thank You!

Val

www.ValTrenda.com

470-219-8031

Contents

Thank You	5
Dedications	11
Intro – The Dream	13
Part 1 – The Want	15
Making the Dream A Reality	22
The Wedding	28
The Reality	40
The Fight	60
Part II – The Ripping	79
The Knock Out	84
The Turmoil	97
Getting To the Light	106
Staying In the Light	114
The Truth about Marriage	120
The Truth about Divorce	130
Notes & Stuff!	137

THANK YOU

Words cannot fathom the amount of gratitude I have for just being one of God's favorites. He has called me His own. So many people have been through the same situation as I and have not come out to tell their story. I thank God for being right by my side the whole time. Even when I thought He had failed me, I later found out that He was holding me in his arms the entire time. Thank you, Lord for allowing me to see this through. Thank you for the strength and thank you for your love. I'm eternally in debt to You because every time I try to repay You with praise and thanksgiving, You show me another side of You and perform another miracle. I can't say thank you enough. If I had 10,000 mouths with 10,000 tongues, it wouldn't even begin the process of expressing my gratitude. I'm in love with You. I trust You. Thank you God!

My Children: words cannot express my gratitude to God for allowing me to be your mother. There were times when I thought I couldn't do the job but you always reminded me that you needed me. I love you both the mostest-er (insider).

Thank you for being patient with me when things were off our normal structure. Thank you for eating cereal for dinner because I was too down or not in the mood to cook. Thank you for giving me the courage to keep going. Thank you for loving me through it all. You will be an awesome man and an awesome woman. Keep up the great work

All three sets of my parents: **My Mother and Stepfather**. You both have been such an inspiration to me. Not only do you support me and my endeavors, but I admire the love that you all share towards God and towards each other. Thank you for being an example to me. Thank you for sheltering me and loving me regardless of my decisions. Thank you for being shoulders to cry on. Thank you for being friends to me. So many children cannot say that their parents are also their friends, but I can! Thank you for your constructive criticism even when I do not want it. (Especially you, Fluffy!!) Thanks for spoiling me and letting me climb in your bed, although I get kicked out after 10 seconds. Thank you for embarrassing me in front of my friends even at the age of 30! Thanks for babysitting. Thanks for the loans. Thanks for the love. Thanks for the prayers. Thanks for EVERYTHING! I love you two more than I did yesterday. And if you read this more than once, I love you more than the day before that too! **My Father and Stepmother**: Thank you for always feeding me. Thanks for being there to listen. Thanks for your support. Daddy, thank you for encouraging me to keep the faith and stay faithful to God. Thank you for checking on me when you knew I was down. Thanks for helping me in my time of need with my car. Thank you for never judging me. I thank the both of you for always praying for me and mostly providing me with so many sisters and brothers to love! ☺ **My**

Godparents: You both have been there for me more times to count. I am so grateful to have the two of you in my life. Thank you for your prayers. Thank you for babying me when I need it. Thanks for allowing me and my children to temporarily live with you during my hardship. I am appreciative for the sacrifice that you had to make for me to stay. I enjoy the dynamics of our relationship. When I need you, you are always there. Thank you for the loans. I am eternally in debt to you because of your generosity. Thank you. To my other set of Godparents, Thank you too for loving me and supporting me throughout all of my years. I love you both dearly.

My Ride or Dies - My sissie Keva, my David-tuh (Richard), baby bookie Delicia, my cousin, who is like a sister to me, TaKeela, my BFF Valerie, bookie-slim Jertoria, my twin Stormi, Sherri, my PhilBee, you all are so important to me. I could have never made it without your phone calls, visits, text messages, encouragements, love and support. Thanks for telling me the truth when I did not want to hear it. Thanks for not judging me. Thanks for being that shoulder to cry on. Thanks for wiping my nose and doing stuff ordinary friends wouldn't do like foot massages. Thank you for encouraging me. Thank you for motivating me. Thank you for taking care of me when I was sick. You've babysat for me, you've held my hand, you've laughed with me, you've cried with me, you've listened to my problems over and over again, and you were there! Thanks for sticking around. I'm eternally grateful.

Bishop RaVonda Nesbitt, yes you deserve your own little paragraph. Without your prayers, I would not have had the strength to even think about making it. Many people do not know the impact you have because you are so humble and aren't like most who like to steal the shine. It all started with that mantle. Although it has been a road to travel, I would do it all over again…I think. Thank you for driving all the way to Tampa just to be at my graduation party. Thank you for keeping your promise. I love you so much for following the voice of God. Thank you for your support and love.

My friends and family: Dionne (with your crazy self, You taught me that it was OK to feel angry but to not stay there-thanks for the support and laughs) "Dem Ones" (Keisha, Keisha and Renea), Brian, Keith, Shameka, Jenna, Justin, All 14 of my siblings including my baby brother Stephon, my baby sister Maria, my big sisters Sharteia, Tangela and Ashley, thanks for being there. All of my aunts and cousins from The Randolph family, the Hip'pard family & the Bouler family, I love you all to pieces! Ebonee (you rock!), Miguel, Amanda, Anteous, Artisa, Mashondria, Betty, Darnell, Raysean, Ms. Y Sampson, Meisha, LaShanda, Dara, Maggie D, Deanna, Lancy, Chele, Javis, LaSandra, Michael, Chandrika, LeShanda, Schrice, New Home New Start, Photo Announce it, CCTB, every last one of my clients, Kizzey, Cherica, Tan, James, Tjuni, Yvette, Al, Monica, Sherard,

Ms. Brenda – Thanks for your continued support and thanks for your wisdom and encouragement to write this book. Even though I was scared; you reminded me that God has not given me a spirit of fear. To a host of others, I cannot name every one of you, but if you are reading this book, please know I am grateful for the impact you have had on my life. THANK YOU for your continued support. Words cannot express how grateful I am to have you apart of my life.

My H.C.C. family: All of the members of Collegiate 100 and Phi Theta Kappa that served with me, thanks for the memories and the lasting friendships! My professors that encouraged me throughout this process thank you. I especially thank all of the professors in the C&HS program, man, I love you people! I'll be back to teach. I will keep that promise.

My previous church fam: I love you all with all my heart. I appreciate everything you have done for me. I appreciate every lesson and every gift. I am grateful to have spent the time with you that I did. You are still my family. May God continue to bless you all!

My Ekk fam....guys, you have no idea how the love you showed me help save my life. Every last hug, every pat on the back and every prayer you sent up, I thank you! Co-pastor LaToya, thanks for those smiles. They would often make my week. Thank you for your push. Thank you for assisting my pastor in ministry. Pastor Major!!!!! Dude, you are awesome. You listen to every cry. I'm sure I would wipe the wind out of you every time you prayed for me. I'm grateful. Thanks for being there. Thank you for taking me in. Thank you for being so overprotective too, (side eye). You looked me in my eye and made me a promise and until this day, you are still upholding it. Thank you for not… letting… me… die!

Dedications

This book is dedicated to the most important person in my life right now, myself. Be healed ValTrenda! I also dedicate this book to all those who have faced divorce and still dealing with the residue. May this book help and guide you into healing. Last but not least, I dedicate this book to my maternal grandmother Barbara Randolph whom I know is shouting and dancing with our Savior in heaven. I miss you and love you so much.

Disclaimer: This book is not for the bashing of men, my ex or marriage or divorce in general. It is simply *my story* from *my perspective* and *my experiences* to assist others. Not everyone's experience was, is, or will be like mine, however it is my desire that you be strengthen and encouraged!

INTRO – THE DREAM

It is every little girls dream to have her Barbie doll life style. She dreams of having the huge house, the white picket fence, the dogs and the children. She even dreams of having multiple cars and barbeques in the back yard. At some point she often dreams of how large her wedding diamond will be. However, out of all the dreams she have, she dreams of having a husband. She dreams of being married to the richest, handsomest, tallest guy she can imagine.

This little girl begins to live out this dream and play it out by way of her baby dolls and toys. She carefully dresses the dolls. She makes them up. She brushes their hair and prance them around the house pretending that she is a good wife. For most young girls, it is the norm.

After the age of 10, the dream begins to turn into reality. All the thoughts of a boyfriend start to fester and come to the surface. She begins to take interest in little Johnny that sits next to her, or when little Matthew plays tag with her, she giggles a little more than she did before. She begins to see that knight in shining armor in a different light. The situation soon turns from him coming to save a woman from a burning tower that's been compromised by dragons and witches, to him coming to her school, playing tag with her and throwing dirt in her hair.

The young lady then begins to set up her expectations of a man. She begins to write out her "man wish list". This list contains her wants and requirements of what she wants in a man. I have never met a woman who did not write out her list! The list included both realistic and unrealistic wants. I believe being rich was on the top of every little girls list. Some wanted a man who was funny while others wrote out lists that included him having a good job, loving his mother and being a great father.

PART 1-THE WANT

My personal list wasn't very long. I believe I've always been different from the normal young lady. Growing up a tomboy, I didn't spend too much time writing out how I wanted to spend my life, but I was sure of how I wanted my future husband to be. I wanted him to be tall, light-skinned, be a great father and have Christian values. I was brought up in a very strict church, therefore having a relationship with Christ was a necessity. It was a very important requirement that was instilled in me as a young girl so I know that it was a prerequisite for my future husband to have.

When I was about 12 years old, I met a young man named James that I just knew I was going to marry. We were raised in the same church and we shared the same values. He was just my type. I thought he was the finest thing that ever walked this planet. Even though I was only 12, I fell in love the moment I laid eyes on him. No, I'm lying. I begin to like him the moment I laid eyes on him, but the moment I fell in love with him, was when he came to talk with me for the first time. He had the most beautiful brown eyes I had ever seen and his voice, oh my, was so calming and relaxing. His heart for God at such a young age really drew me to him. He could sing too. What more could I ask for? I knew that I wanted to be with him forever. My list was very short and he appeared to meet all the requirements.

I remember praying when we were not in each other's company; "I know I'm young, but I would really like to be his wife when I get older." He was so nice and sweet to me. We talked like what seemed like adult conversation at the time. We wrote each other letters and would pass them through mutual friends. We lived miles apart, so we didn't see much of each other. We did not consider ourselves "girlfriend and boyfriend" until I was in high school.

I remember asking an older lady in our church at the time, what love really felt like. I asked her to explain to me how she felt when she knew that her current husband was the one for her. She began explaining her experience and all I can remember is the glow that came upon her face as she began talking about their relationship. However, she did admit that she didn't like him at all when they first met. Even when she was spoken to by God, she didn't want to believe it. Two things stuck out to me when the conversation ended: 1. I wanted that glow she exuded. And 2. I wanted God to speak to me like He did to her.

Speaking with her gave me something to look forward to. So, I began to pray harder. I did not want to lose this guy. I prayed daily. At a young age, I developed a close relationship with my Lord. I could hear Him speak to me. I felt his spirit just like anyone else. I remember reading that

God would give me the desires of my heart. My desire was to b
From a young girl, I wanted to be a wife and mother like my grandmother taught me.

Many people said I was too young to like him so much. My parents did not know how strong my feelings were for him. My dad, forget it! There was no way I would still be alive if he knew that I liked a guy that much and he knew about it. My mother knew of him, but at the time, I was residing with my father so my mother and I did not speak much about that type of stuff. One night while I was getting ready for church, I was ironing my clothes. I was in the middle of my room and I heard a voice as clear as day say, "I will give you to him". I thought I would wet my pants! I had finally received the answer to my prayer, my dream.

I did not share this with anyone but my childhood best friend, Lamar. Lamar was about the only person I could trust with this information because I knew he would not judge me or call me crazy. I knew that God had spoken to me. I knew that James and I were going to be married. We were going to grow up and be with each other forever. All of my childhood dreams of being a wife and mother were that much closer to me. Later down the line, I shared this information with James. He told me that he would be speaking with God for himself. He thought we were way too young to be talking about such a huge life decision. Even though I agreed, I still thought that we should discuss it and start planning our lives together. Such details like: where we ould live and how many children we would have was really important and should be discussed because *I heard the voice of God.*

When I was young and being that I was brought up in the church, I was taught it was "better to marry than to burn" which is found in 1 Corinthians 7:9. When the Pastor would get up and preach about fornication to the young folk that is all we heard! Marry or Burn! So, it was drilled in my head over and over. What they failed to inform us is what the scripture really said. It was instruction given by the Apostle Paul that the preference was for people to stay single like him; however if you were burning with lust and could not control your sexual desires, then get married. I was still a virgin and it was my plan to stay that way until I was married. So, you can see why I wanted to rush and marry, right? As I matured in Christ, I realized that there are other alternatives like disciplining the flesh through fasting and praying to solve the burning with passion issue. Unfortunately, I did not get that lesson until later in life.

A few years later, I believe I caught sight of what James was saying about us being so young. We should enjoy life and our youth. So, I made the decision to end the 'relationship' so that I could freely see others. I remember him saying, "If God told you that you were going to be my wife, why are you ending this-maybe you did not hear from God like you thought." Boy did that hurt. I realized that my decision was not the best one. I spent a lot of time trying to get what James had from others. It was useless. He was one of the most amazing persons I had ever met.

We spent the rest of our teenage and early adult years keeping in touch and occasionally seeing each other. I tried often, several times actually, to rebuild what I knew what was supposed to be, but James was not having it. He soon went off to college and built a relationship with another young lady. I was a bit bothered but I was not too concerned because I had another on and off relationship with another guy I met when I was younger. I was still holding on to the fact that he and I would be married. One day during my senior year in high school while preparing for graduation, I received a call from James. He broke news to me that he was going to be a father. I thought my heart was going to explode. I knew then that he and I would never be together. All hope I had in what this could be was wiped out with only a few words from the other end of my cell phone. My dream of being a wife to this man was shattered. I recalled the night I was ironing my clothes and heard the voice of God. I thought to myself, "Was I mistaken? What happened here?" I was devastated. I felt like a chunk of my heart was taken out and thrown into my hands.

There was only one other guy I that I genuinely cared about and I was under the impression that he did not want to be with me. I used to think I was the reason he enlisted in the military because of all my talk about marriage! So, there I was broken, alone and confused. I knew I heard the voice of God. I knew it! There was nothing that could make me doubt it. I dreamt it. I could even smell the flowers on my wedding day. Not anymore. All I smelled was loneliness and hurt. I blamed myself for this. Guilt lingered around with me for weeks, even years! Even though He was the one having a child from another woman, I felt guilty. I felt like I should have never broken it off with him. He tried to comfort me some time later by telling me we both made our choices and he took part of the blame too, but I knew it was my fault why we were not going to be together.

What do you do when the dream of being something great washes away in front of you? I think a piece of me died after that. My ability to believe what God had told me was beginning to shake. I was beginning to question what I heard God say. "Did God really speak to me? Would God lie to me?" I asked those questions to myself because I was confused and hurt. Why would God allow this? If James was really my future husband wouldn't the plans of God fan out the way they should regardless? I guess not. I was haunted by this for a while. It really was not the fact that I could not be with James. It was mainly because I thought I had a clear ear for God's voice.

It was not until later that I realized that we can mess up plans that God has for us by simply putting our flesh in the way. It is not that God lied or that I did not hear the voice of God, it was that I simply let my own selfish will get in the way of the plans God had for my life. Then God had to go and re-write his plan for my life. God allows us to get in the way of His plan due to free will.

MAKING THE DREAM A REALITY

It was a month after graduation and the death of my grandmother. All I wanted to do was sleep and eat. I was depressed, sad and always hungry. I went to hang out with a friend of mine one day. I must have looked really bad because she kept staring at me. I began to tell her about my sleeping and eating habits and she said "Cherry, you are pregnant". (Cherry is a nickname that was given to me in early middle school). I remember blowing her off and disregarding what she said. It was three weeks after that the walk-in clinic in Town and Country confirmed this.

The pain I felt that day could not be described. As the nurse begin to tell me what my options were, I believed I had an outer body experience. I remember hearing her voice, but not being able to make out what she was saying. Thoughts were flying through my head. In all of my eighteen years of living, I had not ever felt so low. I felt like such a failure. How could I let this happen? How could I have been so naïve and careless?

I wanted to die. I felt like all my dreams and all my aspirations were gone. I flashed back only months before this day to when I was saying my goodbyes to my fellow classmates. I was signing yearbooks and taking pictures and telling everyone to look out for me because I was going to be on their movie and television screens. My passion was acting. I wanted to be a famous movie star. Well, that dream was out the door.

"Ms. Hip'pard? Are you alright?" The nurse asked me, waving her hand in my face in attempt to get my attention. I was dazed out. I do not remember how long I was out or even what was discussed. The next thing I remember is walking home from the clinic. I normally took the bus, but since I know that I needed some time to think, I walked about seven miles back to my home.

The walk home could be compared to the walk of shame. Shame was like a blanket covering my entire body. I wanted to die. As I was walking, thoughts of death taunted me. It was not long before my feet literally began to travel from the sidewalk to the main road. There were cars approaching me as I was walking opposite direction of the traffic. I remember vaguely hearing the horns honking at me. The sounds then became louder and louder. I rushed back to the sidewalk, panting like a pet. I did not realize that I was about to commit suicide that very moment. Not only myself, but the little baby inside of me was going to join me in this horrific moment.
I had a lot of time to think along that stride. Finally, I came to a conclusion that I was going to abort the child. As I got closer to the house, I thought about where the money was going to come from. Surely not my parents. They would probably just rather murder me. I flipped my thoughts back and forth about what conclusion I should come up with. I do not believe that I

ever positively came to a conclusion. The only thing I was sure of is that my parents were going to kill me.

I knew I was going to bring shame to my family. They all had such high hopes for me. Everyone knew my passion for acting, my drive for leaving Tampa, FL and going straight to Hollywood, CA. When I finally arrived at my house, my mother and step-father were at work. I picked up the phone and dialed my Godmother's number. I could not bear to break the news to my mother yet. My Godmother took the news calmly. Although she had several "I told you so's" to release, she was rather composed. The next phone call I made was not to my mother. It was to my step-father. He was the disciplinarian of the family, so I knew he would be mad. I am the type of person that can deal with others being mad at me over others being disappointed in me. That is the feeling I knew my mother would feel.

To my surprise, the sound in his voice was not of anger, but of discontent as well. We both released the phone call and I went to my room to cry. A few moments later, the phone rang. I answered it and it was my mother. My heart sank. My step-father had called her and given her the news. To no avail, she was disappointed. I asked her if she was upset with me. She informed me that she was not upset or mad but she confirmed her feelings of disappointment. I went to my room after hanging up the phone with her and cried even harder. "I cannot have this baby," I thought. "There is no way I can let this family down." I was later talked into keeping the baby.

On February 13, 2002 at 3:52pm, I birthed a baby boy into this world. I named him Jaden. My godmother picked out his name for several reasons. One reason was because I am crazy about Will Smith and He named his son Jaden. The other reason was because it means "God has heard". He was and still is a blessing to me.

Jaden's father initially informed me that he wanted to be involved and he would be there to support me and his child. He told me that I could have an abortion and we could start a family later in life if I felt that would be best for us, but he stressed the fact that he wanted this child and he wanted us to be a family.

The night my son was born, Jaden's father showed up to the hospital. I had chosen to end our relationship toward the end of my pregnancy. He was not too thrilled about that given the fact he wanted us to be a family. Therefore, he began to distance himself from me. When I was released from the hospital, he brought his family to my house to meet baby Jaden. They brought gifts and money. That was the last time I saw them for years to come. No contact from them. No pop up visits from them. There were times that I would call him and cry. I would ask him why he deserted and left without any warning. I knew that it had to be painful to him because he and I were not a couple anymore. I was hurt also, but I was more so distraught at the fact that he begged to have this child only to leave us in the cold. I began to have ill feelings towards my son's father. Every time I would have to sit up at 3:00am or 4:00am holding my child and parenting him because of an earache or a high fever, I would curse his father.

At one point, I was willing to give the relationship another try. I needed a father for my son. I would sacrifice my wants and needs for the sake of my child to be in a home with two parents. I did not want my son growing up without male leadership. My son's father may not have been the best person in the world, but he was the person I decided to have a child with and there was no turning around from that.

When we spoke on the phone about our future, I informed him that I was ready to be in a relationship with him again. I told him that I wanted us to be a family. I said all the right words to get him to do what he needed to do for his son. That is what we do as mothers. We sacrifice ourselves for our children. He agreed. It was under one condition; that I moved to another state with him. Immediately, I was in defense. He couldn't even take care of us while we were in the state we were in and then he wanted to move us to another state? No way! I would not hear of it. He did not have a plan, a job or even a vehicle to get us there. I could not risk it. I freaked out and immediately responded "No". After not hearing from him for a while, I ran into an old mutual friend of ours that informed me that my son's father had moved away. He indeed left and abandoned me and our son.

Real life set in real quick. I was 18 years old, a single mother and alone. Although I had to utilize the system to get assistance to support my son and me, it was certainly not my plan to remain there for the rest of my life. I moved from my godparent's house to my maternal grandmother's house. As soon as I could, I began working as a shift manager at a restaurant. I worked full time and I worked hard. Not long after that, I enrolled at a community college to try and make something of myself. I would leave my full time job, go and pick up my son from one day care and take him straight to another which at times consisted of friends helping me out. I went to school twice a week.

    I had to show the world I could make it, that I could survive this life change. I refused to be another statistic. I had to prove everyone wrong who said that I was a failure for being so bright and getting pregnant right out of high school. Not to mention having a baby out of wedlock. The Christian community did not welcome having babies outside of marriage. Although a lot of the Christians who made such a hassle about it were the main ones who were having sex out of wedlock, they just didn't have the evidence in the form of a child. A lot of Christians had made the same mistake I made and quite honestly, still do.

THE WEDDING

I rededicated my life back to God. I really wanted to be in love with God. I needed to be in love with God. I was alone. If there was anything I learned from my upbringings, it was that I needed God in my life. He would prevent me from sinning and help me with any issue I was dealing with. I was raised in the Pentecostal church. To be more specific, I was raised in the apostolic belief. It is my opinion that in the Pentecostal belief, there was a lot of "do not do this. Do not do that. Do not go here or there. Do not say this and do not say that. Do not dress this way and definitely do not dress that way." Therefore, I felt a lot of pressure from the Christian community regarding my situation. Sure enough, I did not have a husband. I did not even have an active baby daddy!

When news hit about my pregnancy and even after my son was born, I felt others looking at me funny. I felt that people were laughing at me. I felt that my family was so disappointed in me that they shunned me. In fact, when my father's girlfriend, who is now my step-mother told my father I was pregnant, he went ballistic. I remember I went to visit my father shortly after he received the news and he would not even look me in the eye. I walked into his house and He walked right pass me. I said "Dad, aren't you going to give me a hug?" My father responded, "You don't deserve a hug". That was the most hurtful thing I had ever heard my father say to me. I heard some pretty mean comments from others about my pregnancy and the baby, but that by far was the most detrimental. My dad later forgave me after a fall-out phone conversation between the two of us. My belief is that he was extremely hurt and did not know how to express it.

I hid myself in different activities in the church so that I would not have to date but I secretly knew I wanted to. I knew I wanted to be with someone. I met a friend at the church who is currently my best friend. Her name is Keva. She, along with some other young ladies at the church I attended began to get engaged left and right. I mean, every time one turned their head, there was a proposal of marriage. I began to get sick to my stomach. All of these young ladies, some still in their teens, were snatching up these men like hot cakes. I thought to myself, "What are they doing that I am not?" I wanted what they were getting. I wanted the proposal. I wanted the ring and I definitely wanted the wedding!

About ten months after my son was born I began to date. I had a list of requirements that I thought I wanted in a man but I wanted to be married so badly that some of them went out the door. As I would go to dinner with some of these guys, one of my first questions was "so, what your thoughts are about marriage?" Here I am, only 19 years of age, the ink still wet on my high school diploma and no college degree and all I wanted to talk about was marriage because the church folk taught me that it was better to marry than to burn. Not only was I burning but everywhere I walked the heat would set something afire. However, that was not my main concern. My main concern for getting married was because I needed a father for my son. My second concern was that of my religious views and how I was perceived being a single mother. My third concern was that everyone was doing it. It sounds juvenile but it is the truth.

    I ran a lot of guys off with my marriage question. One of the main reasons I believe is because I was young. No one wanted to get married at 19 years old. That was not the most popular thing to do. But what else could I do? I was feeling so left out. Most of my friends from high school were in college or doing their own thing and the new friends I met at my new church were all getting married. So I was left alone. Instead of waiting and realizing that marriage was way more serious than doing it because everyone else was doing it, I wanted what I wanted. However, my reason for wanting it was not solely because of everyone else. I wanted stability and a father for my son.

    I dated this guy and I now see that I was trying to force marriage on him. I wanted him to meet my parents. I wanted him to come to all of the family socials. I wanted him to help me with my son. I can admit I was a bit determined. He would always decline. We saw each other for a few months. One day I went to call him and he did not answer. He abruptly stopped talking to me. This happened several times with others. But it did not stop me. The way I saw it, I needed to break this statistic. I did not want to be another African American single mother with no college education and more specifically, no husband. How could one have a family as a single mother?

There was this young man who worked with me at the store I managed. In fact, we both went for the hourly shift manager position at the same time and were promoted together. He was tall, handsome and from a different country so he had an accent. I remember the first time I saw him. I entered in the store to start my shift and there he was sitting in the lobby eating his lunch. He looked directly in my eyes, yet I kept walking ahead. He had been out of work for a few weeks due to medical reasons. Therefore, I did not get a chance to meet him when I first started at the store. My fellow coworkers introduced him to me as Lance. I heard a lot of great things about him so I imagined he was a pretty decent guy. I did not pick up interest in him while we were coworkers. He was married. Nonetheless, we got along and worked well together.

Not long after we were promoted, the area managers of our store transferred Lance out to another location. We would only see each other occasionally. At times, he would call my store to handle business or vice versa. One day, I was asked to work at a different store to fill in for another manager. This was not abnormal. While ending my shift, another manager came to take over, it was Lance. We joked, laughed some and soon after, we handled business. I ended my shift that Friday night and headed home. Later that night, a friend of mine invited me to go out with her. There was this night club called "Joy" that was pretty popular. I worked hard that week and thought I could use the night out.

While out dancing, I see Lance enter the dance floor. Shocked, I look at him and smiled. He walked over and gave me a hug. We chatted shortly about work and he offered to purchase me a drink. I accepted. When he came back with my beverage, we short talked. I thanked him and he walked over. Soon after, Lance came back around my way and asked to dance with me. My response was "Sure."

We danced almost the entire night. I remember smiling as I left the night club thinking "what just happened? I don't even like him like that."

I went to work the next day. Early that Saturday morning one of my employees picked up the phone and told me I had a call. It was Lance. He told me that he needed to come by my store to handle some business. He asked if I wanted him to bring me something to eat. I smiled. There is a saying that states, "The way to a man's heart is through his stomach". I believe that statement is meant for me as an exception. I replied, "Yes."

We soon began to date for several months. This was not an easy process. The fact remained: He was still legally married. I rationalized my reason and decided to date him because I knew that he and his wife were separated since he was working at the store with me. I felt that since it was over between them, it was ok. I was wrong for my decision. I would later suffer the consequence for that decision.

Lance was very generous. One thing I loved about him was his ability to be so kind. He would lend out money to his friends and never received it back. I would fuss at him all the time because I knew people was taking advantage of him. He would give people car rides and not ask for anything. His smile always warmed my heart. He was a provider. This was a trait that was number one on my list. Every female knows what "the list" is. He took care of me and my son. Lance made sure that whatever my son and I needed we would have it at his expense. He was also very attentive. He loved to hug and kiss. He would often caress my face and tell me I was beautiful.

Lance got along with my son, my family and my friends. He did not have any children of his own and his family did not live in the same city or state as us. Therefore, he was able to spend a lot of time with me and my son. He would get off work and come straight to my house. We did a lot of things together. He would take us to the park, to the movies and shopping. We even traveled together. I asked him to come to church with me and he agreed. He saw how happy the people were to be in church and praising God. He told me after a few visits that he wanted that same excitement for God and he wanted to be saved. Not long after that, He received Christ as his personal savior.

Being that I was not interested in him initially, the question did not come up quickly about marriage like it did with the others I had dated. But I began to like him. He was rather persistent. His determination and will to assist me in life is what won me over. Essentially, to be my partner in making this life thing work is what he would become.

One day I had to work my shift and I did not have a babysitter for my son. Lance was off that day. He volunteered to watch my son for me. While I was appreciated the tenacity and the courage it took for him to volunteer, I was skeptical. I was uncertain that he could actually carry out taking care of my son for a whole eight hours. I knew that he was trying to get to know my son, but he was also trying to get in good with me also by helping me out. Against my doubtfulness, I allowed him to keep my son. I called them every hour on the hour. I'm sure I was annoying, but I did not care because my main concern was my child. When I returned, my son was left in one piece and Lance was worn out.

We dated for about four months and then we began the serious talk. We talked about where we would live, if we would have more children and how we wanted our future to be. Everything seemed to be right. Everything seemed to me that it would work out. When I look back at it, it seemed like a business arrangement.

One night after leaving my parent's house, we drove a different way home. He pulled over abruptly. He got out of the car and came around to the passage side. He bent down and was checking out the tire. Still sitting in the car, I waited for him to tell me what was wrong. My son was in the back seat, we were both clueless. He yelled to me, "get out of the car and come look at this!" When I got out of the car, he was on his knee with the ring in his right hand. He said to me, "Look over there." He pointed to the sign "Joy". We were in front of the club that we danced all night in some months back. He began his speech and eventually asked me to marry him. My response was "yes".

I returned home and called almost everyone in my phonebook to inform them of the good news. I was so excited. The ring was gorgeous! My close friends and family had already been alarmed of his plan to propose.

The night of his proposal, I sat and thought about how my life was getting ready to change. I thought I was finally getting what I thought I deserve. Someone to assist me through life, help me with my son and love me for whom I was. The only issue was that I was not in love with him. I figured that would come later. At that time, my focus was to have a stable family and get an in house father for my son.

My life did change, dramatically at that. Wedding planning was fun but very irritating and draining. We both worked hard to pay for the wedding. Every pay check, money was going out to cover expenses for this event. I wanted a nice wedding but nothing too vast and extravagant. One day, I was sitting in our room thinking about who would all attend my wedding. I was so stressed out. Lance entered the room after a long day at work and gave me a nice massage. He was so gentle and caring. He would often tell me not to worry and that things would work out.

Our relationship was rather mediocre. We did not have very deep conversations with each other. We did not speak too heavily on important items like politics, religion and things like 401Ks. We just wanted to be married. We talked basic things like what bill was due and who was going to watch my son while we went out on a date. We would often visit my best friend Keva and her husband. We spent a lot of time around my friends and had what I would like to call regular conversations about kids, bills and taking care of the family.

After getting the list together as to who would be in my wedding, I asked my roommate at the time to be a part of this important event. Initially she agreed but one day she came to me and said something that eventually hurt me. She informed me that she could not be a part of my wedding because she did not feel that it was right. According to her, Lance was not saved and she did not want to be a part of joining together what is called in Christendom, the "unequally yoked". I was devastated. I thought, "Why should it matter? You are not God. Ultimately it is my decision who I want to marry". Needless to say, she dropped out of my wedding. In fact, she did not even attend the event as a guest even though she was invited. Even though she hurt me, I forgave her and we later on down the line made up.

Eventually my roommate moved out. My son and I stayed in the apartment for some time. As I got deeper into the wedding planning, finances were cutting short. Lance and I decided that it would be best if he moved in with us. We did not tell many people because I was taught that you should not live together before you were married. The older people called it "shacking". It's a term meant to describe a male and female who are interested in each other or dating that reside in the same house and they are not married. The older people, mainly church people, said that it was a sin to shack. I later found out through my own research and understanding that it is not a sin, it just puts you in a higher position to sin. Although I felt bad, I still felt that as a grown woman, I made my own decisions.

As time got closer to wed, I would question my decision to marry him. I thought it was cold feet. I should have looked further into it then. He would want to kiss and touch me all the time and I would become so annoyed. I would ask myself why I would be so annoyed at something that I liked. Who would become annoyed at such affection? It was not the affection. It was him. I was not in love. Sure, I loved him. I cared great deal for him, but I was not in love. I lied. I lied to him. I lied to my family and most importantly, I lied to myself. I was in love at the thought of being married. I was in love with the fact that someone would now be here to help me. I was in love with the security.

One day I was exiting the restroom of my apartment and I clearly got a feeling something was wrong. I paused. I stood straight in the doorway of the restroom and just waited. I had no idea what was going on. I waited more. I soon discerned the spirit of God warn me that I was not to marry him. God speaks to us all differently. He spoke to me with discernment. It was an indescribable feeling. I continued to stay and wait. I had no idea what I should do. I was frozen. Here it is only months away from my wedding date and I feel that I am not supposed to marry him? I began to walk off. I remember physically shaking off the feeling. I ignored it. I ignored God. I was certain that I felt the spirit of God and I knew exactly what I was told, but I ignored it like a rich man walking pass a bum on the street.

I was thrown back to the thought of what my ex-roommate told me. I was not about to prove her right or any of them for that matter. Yes, indeed there were people who did not want me to marry. It was not that they did not like Lance, but it was their own personal reasons. I did consider the things some said, but it was not enough to move my decision. Even in counseling with our pastor, I considered it yet I did not budge.

With only five weeks left before my wedding to take place, I was informed by my doctor that I was only weeks pregnant. The small fear of if I should get married or not disappeared. No way was I going to call the wedding off now and be stuck yet again with another baby father to deal with. No. I needed a husband at this point. I thought about how life would be as a single mother of two. No husband. No education. Here I was again tortured by this thought. I soon ended that torture when I said "I do".

On May 22, 2004, we were married at our home church. We had a traditional church wedding. I was elated. The feeling in the waiting area was euphoric. I could not wait to meet him at the altar. In the pews, my family and friends were there to support me. They were all there to witness such a vow. Strolling down an aisle of petals and gentle music, my step-father and father gave me away. Underneath soft lighting and candles, I repeated the words that my pastor instructed. I stood before God and made a vow to Him and to my soon to be husband. A vow that I would later break.

THE REALITY

Everything was great. I was married. I had a father for my son. I was content. The lessons my grandmother and mother taught me about being a good wife and mother were starting to kick in. I began to take pride in being a wife and mother. I cooked at least four meals a week. I kept a clean house. I worked a full time job as well, so it was not an easy task. However, I knew how to get the mission accomplished.

My husband had no complaints. Well, at first. But who complains the first year of marriage? That's why it's called the honeymoon stage. There was limited fighting so we pretty much got along well. On November 21, 2004, I went into labor in church and was rushed to the hospital. I birthed Janiya into this world at 3:52pm, the same exact time my son was born. This, of course, added to my contentment. Our daughter was born healthy, my son was happy and my mother-in-law had moved in with us to help out. What more could a girl ask for?

Soon after we married, it became a struggle for me to carry the household alone. Lance was not raised to help out around the house. In fact, he had maids help care for him. He had tons of sisters and a very generous mother. He was used to women catering to him left and right. Now, I had no problem catering to my husband. However, I needed some assistance. Although his mother resided with us and helped out, there were some things that were to be completed by the hands of a man. For instance, I would have to pull teeth to get him to remember the trash days. That may seem small for some but if one person is taking care of a full three bedroom, two bathroom house, it could be a lot. I would have to remind him about the cars needing to be washed and the grass needed to be cut. It was like taking care of another child. However, we managed the best way we could.

I learned quickly that taking care of a household, being a wife and a mother was not as easy as I thought. There were lessons I had to learn every day. I had to learn to submit. I had to learn patience. I had to learn what battles to fight and which to leave alone. I had to learn about jealousy on both our parts. I mainly had to learn about living out the vows I made to God and my husband in front of all those people.

The reality in submitting is the requirement of both parties. The misconception is that only the woman is required to submit. This is incorrect knowledge according to the bible (Ephesians 5:21). I wanted to please my husband. Therefore, I did what he wanted me to do feasibly . If he wanted me to stay home instead of going out with my friends, mainly I did. I will not state that it went down like that all the time, but for the most part I would stay home if he asked.

Submitting became difficult when we joined another church and his interest in church declined. I became active in our new church rather swiftly. I wanted to do work for God, so I jumped in full force to help out the ministry. I was on the praise team, I became the church secretary, and then I slowly entered into ministry by preaching the gospel. There were a few Sunday mornings I would get everyone's clothes ready for church, make breakfast and feed everyone. Lance would still be in the bed. After I would serve him breakfast in bed, I would ask him if he was going to attend church. Several times, he would say no. I would get so frustrated. It was like he lost all interest in going to church and in worshipping God.

There were plenty of fights when it came down to church. I often asked him what happened to his zeal. I questioned whether it was all a front to get to me. I hoped it was not. However, it was clear that he was not interested in church anymore. I would still attend church. It was difficult having to explain to folks that would ask me where he was. Of course, I could not lie. So I would always smile and say that he was tired from work so he stayed home. All the while, I would be burning up inside. Not only at the fact that he was not there and I felt he should have been but the fact that these people would ask me questions about him and I had to put up a front. I made it seem like everything was fine and my marriage was great. When the truth was I was always frustrated.

I would be so aggravated with Lance. It seemed to me that he depended on me to do everything for him. I ironed his clothes. I cooked all of his meals and served them to him. I cleaned up behind him. I fixed things in the house that normally a man would do. For example, once the kitchen dishwasher had broken in our house. I sat up trying to fix it while he was in the bedroom snoring. His philosophy was to call someone and pay them to fix it. I wanted to save money and I was just under the impression that that is what men do, they fix things. My father was a hard worker and he would fix things around the house some times. However, he would call people to fix things as well. My stepfather, it would basically have to be the house caving in before he called someone to fix anything before him. He taught me that no matter what you have, it is yours and you must take care of it because it is yours! I took that seriously. I liked to take care of my things. But not Lance, he left it up to me to handle all of those things.

Regardless of what went on in our household, I still submitted to him. I felt that I was still a good wife. I would still cater to him left, right, up and down. He was my husband and the way I saw it, I had to do what I had to do to keep him my husband. I prayed day and night for our marriage. I wanted it to work. I was so young and with a small baby and a toddler, it was challenging to keep up my marriage to him. No matter how angry I was with him, when he wanted to have sex, I never denied him. He had a high libido and denying him was not what I was taught. It did not matter about how I felt, how sad I was, how disappointed I was, or if whatever the problem was had even been solved, as long as I did not deny him, I was ok.

Being a new wife was not all I thought it was cracked up to be. It was work. When I say it was work, that's what I mean! I would work a full time job and come home and still have another full time job to attend to. When everyone went to sleep, that's when I worked on things for the ministry. At times, I would be so exhausted that I waited until Sunday morning to do the church's work. Anything for me, anything personal, was out of the question. I had no time.

I soon learned to have patience with Lance. I would pray and pray for God to help us. I would read the bible and read stories about wives and mothers. I was introduced to the book by Stormie Omartian, *"The Power of a Praying Wife"*. I was doing everything in my power to keep my part of the vows up. Therefore, I began to try to help him. I wanted him to be this righteous and upright person as my stepfather or my pastor at the time. I compared him to these powerful men that I saw and had the pleasure of seeing them as a husband or as a man of God that cherished his relationship with Christ. I wished that Lance was like them.

The truth is, had I spent more time dating and courting him, I would have found out a lot about Lance. We would fight. Not physically but verbally. We would scream and yell at each other. We both appeared to be rather bossy and a tendency to control so we had to have the last word.

Therefore, arguments with Lance would last hours, sometimes days. There were times where we would only speak to each other when we had to. We would still greet each other with a kiss but, it was would be so quick and unemotional that a stranger would think we were just brother and sister and not husband and wife. I had to suffer the consequences and go through my marriage like a big girl.

Only a year after being married, I could not take it anymore. I had never been in such a serious relationship as an adult. Some of these situations I had to face were surreal to me. They were foreign. I did not know how to handle them. I would become so irritated. In fact, I was always irritated. It began to affect my work. I could hardly concentrate on being a supervisor at the job I was working on. Prayer did not seem to be working.

I did not want my marriage to end. I wanted support. I wanted comfort and I wanted someone to tell me that I was worth more than what I was receiving. I was not receiving what I thought I should have. I thought I should have been receiving a lot more appreciation, attention and validation. I wanted Lance to tell me how grateful he was to have me as his wife. I wanted him to be there for me when I was sick. I wanted him to help me around the house more often. I was so tired of doing all of the work in the house and in the marriage. I had to hold up the family and be the protector and the care taker. It was so exhausting. I wanted someone to slap him to tell him to straighten up and do what I wanted him to do and be how I wanted him to be. I felt that I worked hard at being a good wife but he did not work hard at being a good husband. Although I was not in love, I did love him and did not want to hurt him.

I was only 23 years old at the time. I was soon fired from my job so my fulltime job became a housewife. Things at home were getting tight. My mother in law worked and helped as much as she could. Ultimately, the pressure turned to Lance to provide for his family. I did the best that I could to try and keep peace with him. I knew how hard it had to be for him to provide for us and make sure we had what we needed. I was sure that he was under a lot of stress. Therefore, I would make sure that everything was done at home so that he did not have to do anything.

Soon, his pressure cooker top began to blow. He was short tempered a lot of the times. He would come home and half speak to everyone in the house. I knew something more was bothering him because he would say that he was tired, but he would leave the house soon after getting in from work and go to his friend's house. This happened often. In fact, it became so regular that I began to make dinner earlier so that it was done when he came home so that if he wanted to leave he could.

After a while, it seemed like it did not matter to him at all whether dinner was ready or not. He would leave anyway. He would not help me with the children. My son was attending preschool and I would be home all day with my daughter and mother in law. My mother in law worked at night.

That meant that by the time night came, he would take my mother in law to work and head to his friend's. I was stuck with being home with both children for the rest of the night without any "down" time. I remember sitting to the dinner table every night for weeks eating with my children alone. It was torture. I was married, had a family and was as alone as a prisoner in solitary. At times, I was so lonely, I would fall asleep in my son's room. I could not take the torment any longer. I knew my marriage was not all I wanted it to be. I knew that I was not always the best wife. He would often accuse me of cheating and was jealous a lot of the times. Yet and still, I wanted my marriage. I wanted to be happy. Thus, I became desperate for things to get better.

  I was at the church doors before the doors even opened. I was at every bible study and at every Sunday morning service. I would be the first one at every church event. I would be waiting on the minister or the pastor to come and unlock the door. My marriage was a mess. My husband did not have any interest in church anymore. I was working in the church to hide what was going on in my marriage and to stay out of trouble.

  Soon, I went to my pastor. I told him some of the things that were happening with me and Lance. He suggested counseling. Lance was not having it. The way Lance saw it, we did not have a problem. He said the only problem was that I needed to stop working so much for the church because that was the real issue. He even suggested that we return back to the church we were attending when we got married. It was a much larger church than the one we moved membership to. I did not work for the larger church, thus the reasoning for him wanting to go back to the previous ministry.

Once my pastor knew this, he stopped me from working for his ministry. He told me that I would need to fix my marriage. He did not want us to be divorced on his watch let alone by reasoning of me working too much for the ministry and my husband unsatisfied about it. Although it deeply hurt my feelings, I understood my pastor's reasoning for doing this. Working for the church was my coping mechanism. It was the way I dealt with everything that was going on. I had nothing going for myself. I was only a wife, a mother and a ministry worker. That's it! My life simply revolved around those three things. Now, one of my roles was taken away from me because of my husband.

I continued to press my way to our church services. My husband attended service with me when he felt like it, which was not that often. Things were not all that bad in our marriage before, but by now, they were worse. I cried every Sunday in church. I would beg God to help me but deep in my mind, I always felt I was getting what I deserved. I felt like it was because I married when I was not supposed to.

Lance would come home from work, take a quick shower and immediate walk right back out the door with only a greeting of hello and one of goodbye. Our greetings would be so emotionless. It was like living with a roommate. He began to only speak to me when it was something of importance. Our conversations were not fulfilled with warmth and genuineness. They were quick and to the point. He was always missing. My mother and I would talk every evening. She would often ask me how were things, like mothers do. When she asked me about Lance, I would always tell her that he was not home. One night she asked me where he was and I told her that he was not there. She appeared upset. She said, "Where is He? How come every night we speak he is never home?" I responded to my mother, "Mother, time will reveal what is going on. Time will reveal."

By this time, I knew exactly what was happening. I heard many people talk about "women's intuition". This is what I figured I had. I knew Lance was having an affair with someone. His attention was not on me. As I mentioned, he was a very sexual person. He was not sleeping with me as much as he was prior. He did not touch me the way he did before. Even in the past when we would fight, he could not last very long without caressing me. He loved to kiss me and compliment me. That soon decreased. His patterns changed. He began to do things that were not in his character. These were the things that allowed me to think there was something wrong. I would call my best friend Keva daily. I would inform her about what was going on so that she could help me get through this. I asked her one day, "Do you think it is because of my weight?" She would often laugh out of amusement from the question. I was not comfortable with my weight at the time. I thought that this could possibly be why Lance was ignoring me. There had to be a valid reason why he was not carrying out his role as my husband. I was doing everything the right way. So, what else could it have been?

This is what spouses of society face. We depend on our spouses to play the role they need to play. We often feel that if we are giving our all, our 100%, then so should the spouse. After all, we are supposed to be in this together, right? The truth is that is not how it always works. Marriage is playing in your role even when the other steps out of theirs. When the one partner gives up on their role in the marriage, the other partner's job is to stay in their role and love that partner back to his or her place. In result, the person who remains in role becomes the transporter of the marriage. They become the baggage carrier. It is now their responsibility to maintain and hold everything together so that everything appears to be in place to the outside world. At times, the spouse that is out of role has no idea that they are out of role. They are sometime so far gone into a new role that the role they should be active in becomes old news and vanishes.

I carried this intuition for about two weeks. I gathered my information. I had never been the type of wife to go through his phone or have to sniff behind his back and go through his things. I wanted him to trust me so I in return trusted him. I felt that was childish to do those things. If I had a reason to, I would. During this time, I felt I had reason to but I was too chicken to confirm what I had been feeling. What was I going to do if I actually confirmed that he was having an affair? Leave? How was I going to support my children? I started a temporary job at a company that paid me well but it was not enough to support me and my children with the lifestyle that we were accustom to living. I could not concentrate on that though. I told myself that I would have to make adjustments to my lifestyle. I was not living a lavishing lifestyle but it was more than I had when I was a single mother. Now, I had two children to care for. Therefore, I put much thought into what I was going to do.

During those two weeks, I tested him. One night when he came home from work, I dressed in lingerie while he was in the shower. Upon his exit, I attempted to entice him. I rubbed his face gently with my fingers. He loved to be caressed and kissed. I kissed him around his neck. I began to show him my lingerie. I smiled and continued to show off myself to him. He looked me square in my face and told me, "Move, I have to go." In disbelief, I slowly moved from in front of him and watched him walk right out of our bedroom door and soon heard the front door slam, next the car door slammed and the engine turned over. I was astonished. I could not believe what had just happened. I flopped on the bed and sobbed like a baby. That was yet and still not enough proof for me, although it should have been.

A few days later, I was giving my daughter a bath. I wanted to call him to see when he would be home because it was getting late. When I called him, he did not answer. I heard the sound of his voicemail which had my voice recording on it. Somehow, I thought about checking his voicemail. I did not know his voicemail password. The way most voicemails are set up, you can check them from a different phone if you push the right button. I proceeded to push the pound button on my landline phone hoping that I could skip the voicemail recording and skip to the beep, but I pushed the wrong button. The automatic voice recording asked me for a password. I paused for a moment and then pushed in the first group of numbers I thought I would be. Just like that, voila, I was in. The recording said "you have two new voicemails." I pushed the numbers to hear them. One of the recordings was of me asking him to hurry home. I pushed the button to keep the message new and the next one came up. I could not believe what I heard. The sounds of that woman's voice on my husband's voicemail freaked me out. I was livid. Then hurt. Then livid again. She stated her name and began to speak about personal things that happened to him over the last week. From the sound of it, she had much knowledge of his personal life. She had excessive emotion in her voice. The sound carried much interest. This was not someone he just met. It appeared to me that this was an ongoing relationship.

    I listened to that voicemail about ten times in a row. I phased out. All I saw was yellow. It was the color of the bathroom walls in the bathroom where I was bathing my daughter. I do not know how long I was mentally gone but when I came to, my daughter was crying for me to get her out of the tub. I immediately pushed the buttons to keep the message in new status as I did the first message. I took my daughter out of the tub and continued my night as a mother. Later on that night he pranced in the door with the smell of disgust. I wanted to knock the color right off his skin. I wanted vengeance. I growled under my breath when he climbed into bed that night. I wanted to pick up the king size mattress we slept on and throw it at him. He rolled over and cupped me with is arms and pulled me near him. I wanted to puke. All I could hear was the sound of her voice in my head. I replayed the message over and over again mentally. Surely I was insane for allowing it to fester but I could not do a thing about it. I was in shock. I could not believe that this was happening. As I laid in his arms that night my eyes filled with tears of anger all the while, he slept peacefully right next to me.

    Thoughts ran across my mind the whole night. I thought about what was going to be my next step. I thought about how I was going to survive if I left him. I thought about if I should even leave him. I was confused. I did not know whether to leave him or stay. I had no direction. I felt stuck. I had no plan. There was nothing inside of me that gave me a feeling of security in this matter. My feelings were all over the place. I was angry. I was hurt. I was embarrassed and I was disturbed.

    I went to work the next day. I contacted my mother and we talked our daily conversation. I did not mention it to anyone. I still needed more information. When I later mentioned this to some girl friends of mine, they told me how crazy I was for not going World War III on him that night but I was not sure what all happened. Granted, I could tell it was more than just a voicemail by his prior actions and the sound of her voice. I continued to do research. About two days later, while he was asleep I built up enough courage to go through his phone. I searched for her name and wrote down her number on a small sticky note. I stuck the paper on the inside top of my nightstand so that no one would find it. During this time, I acted normal. If he wanted to make love, I did. I did not deny him no matter how disgusted I was. Not to mention the fact that I was taking a huge risk. If indeed he was having a full relationship with this woman that included sexual encounters, there was the risk of receiving a STD. Nonetheless, I had no information other than what I heard for myself. All the while knowing what he was up to, I continued to cook for him, clean and complete all of my other household duties. I got tired of faking. I was getting disgusted by the minute.

On one of the nights I knew he would leave. I asked a friend of mine to come over and act like we were going to hang out. She came not long after Lance had gotten home. He completed his normal routine by showering, dressing and kissing me goodbye. This time when he walked out of the door, I waited about ten minutes. I got into my car and drove off in attempt to follow him. I drove over to the house he stated he was at. When I pulled up, I parked across the street and turned off my engine. I waited there for about thirty minutes. My other vehicle, the one that he was driving was not there. The whole time I sat there, he never showed up to where he said he would be. Again, more proof. I came home that night and my friend who babysat for me left. I picked up my phone, went over to my nightstand and did the boldest thing I thought I could do.

She answered the phone, "Hello?" I waited. I was speechless. She sounded twelve! With my talent perfected in Drama class, I pretended to be someone else. I informed her that I was a woman from Lance's job and that his wife knew about their affair and that she would be calling her. I wanted to get a feel for this woman. The woman was shocked that he was even married! She stated that she had no idea. I soon disconnected the phone call and returned the call as myself a few minutes later. I had to call my best friend first. I needed her support. I informed her of what was happening. She, being very protective of me, was livid! However, she managed to stay calm. When this young woman answered the phone it appeared that she had been crying. I began to speak to this woman. She admitted to me where she met Lance, how long they have been in communication with each other and how often they had been sexually intimate and where. With every word she spoke, I wanted to regurgitate all over my bedroom. Then she did something that threw me for a loop. She cried. That action told me that it was more than sex. Well, at least it was for her. It was more of a relationship. The last part blew my mind. She was only 19 years old. I thought, "This man is a fool. Why would you risk your marriage on a relationship with a kid?"

I felt sick. I ended my phone call with this young lady. I did not once yell at her or take any of my frustrations out on her. I asked her myself if she knew He was married and she stated she did not know. Therefore, I could not blame her. I could not act like she was the cause of this. Every ounce of frustration and rage I had was directed at Lance. There are too many women who direct their frustrations toward the woman who their man had an affair with when the real issue is with the partner. Once I determined that she did not know his marital status, I received all the information I needed and moved on.

I went to church that Sunday and I had an experience with God like never before. My husband was not in attendance that day. I needed answers. I needed a green light on this situation I felt the need to stay because I felt like I owed him because *I wasn't in love with him.* I married him for all the wrong reasons. However, I was so low and so beat up with this situation, I had not a clue what to do. I did not think that payback would be this harsh. When I got to church, I cried the entire service. I prayed the entire service. I told God I was not walking out of that church until He did something about that situation. My prayers and tears did not go unnoticed. People came up to me after church to ask if I was ok, but I was in a daze. I left and went home. The next day, that Monday, all Hell broke loose in that house.

We were lying in bed watching TV. My nerves were a wrecking ball. I felt it was time this all came to an end. Finally, I built up the courage to confront him. I asked him out of the blue who this person was. Of course, he became very defensive. He began to deny and scream and yell. I went to go reach for his phone and he pushed me off the bed. I stood up, balled up my fist and socked him in the mouth like Derek Jeter swinging for a homerun. All the anger and frustration I had built up for those past few months and especially those past two weeks released on him in the matter of a sucker punch to the face. He stood in amazement. He left the house after cleaning up his face. I was a mess. I was crying hysterically. The children were sleeping. My mother in law was still working. Needless to say, there was a huge argument upon his return. The more I continued to question him about it, the more he continued to deny it. Eventually, I went to sleep. The next day, I called Keva and told her to pick up my son from school and keep him until things worked out. I knew this was not over. Not even close to being done.

We were home alone in the house the next day. I forced him to speak to me about it. Again, he continued to deny it. After a while, he became silent. It was like he was trying to figure out what to say or how to say it. I thought I would help him out by admitting that I spoke with the young lady and she told me everything. He yet denied it. The whole time, my demeanor was simply to get him to admit to me what happened and what was going on so that we could determine our future. I guess the time I had spent processing this whole thing decreased my anger. Now, I was still angry, but I was able to manage my emotions a lot better than normal. In fact, I thought it was a little too abnormal. I was not crying. I was not yelling. I was very neutral. I just wanted answers so that we could get to a solution. However, he was making it very difficult being that he would not cooperate with me and my questions. Fed up with begging him for information, I walked out of the living room and into our bedroom and I began to pack my clothes. After a while, Lance returned and asked me where I was going. When I told him I was leaving him, he finally admitted to what he had done. He informed me where and how they met, how long it had been going on and how many times he had been sexually involved with her. Needless to say, I completely broke down. I thought I was ready to hear the truth. I was not. No matter of preparation could prepare me to physically see our marriage going down the drain. No matter what wrong I had done or what wrong he had done, our marriage was a disaster. It was a complete mess. It was like a ball of barb wire rolling down a hill.

After long days and days of crying and praying, we agreed that we would work on our marriage. This time I decided to listen spiritually. I followed the voice of God after I clearly heard him tell me to stay and work out my marriage with Lance. Naturally, I felt guilty. I felt that this was payback so I had to suck it up and move on. That's what I did. He called our pastor and told him that he was now ready for counseling. We endured counseling for about six months. Our pastor would meet us at our house and sometimes we would go to his. He and his wife would genuinely pour out their hearts to us to help us get pass this hurt. They were very transparent and honest with us. It took a while for us to get to a place where I thought we should be but with hard work, we began to love each other entirely.

THE FIGHT

After about a year of our stumbling mountain, we figured that we needed a new start. Moving to another city was a thought but we both really wanted to stay in my hometown. I was too frightened to move away from my family given that we had just begun to truly rebuild our marriage. We decided to purchase a house. We moved along with the children and without his mother. It was a gorgeous four bedroom, two bathrooms and two-car-garage Riverview home. I loved it. It was on the end of a cul-de-sac so we did not have much traffic. I loved this because the children could play outside without me worrying to much. We had very kind neighbors that brought treats and goodies when we first moved in. The elementary school my children would attend was graded an A school. I could not ask for more.

We began to continue to work on our marriage. We still had our issues but this time, I had decided to invest my heart into this. I realize now that I viewed and acted upon this marriage as if it were a business plan. My father being a very successful businessman taught me well when it came to business opportunities. I was taught to take on some challenges but go for success. Get the contract or the client so I could make more money. In this case, I looked at it as 'take care of me so I could take care of you.' The funny thing about business plans are that, you very seldom get your heart involved. Business is business. If it fails, do not get your feelings hurt, fix it and deal with it or drop it and move to the next deal. There is no time to waste but there is plenty of time to be successful. That was my way of thinking prior to our huge falling out. I wanted my marriage to succeed so I had to fix it. I had to work on it.

    I began to invest my feelings into this marriage and solely into Lance. I never got the opportunity to really fall in love with Lance. I learned to love him. As time went on, I loved him through the love of God. God told me I had to love, so that's what I did. My pastor taught me through the word of God how to love Lance. I read the biblical stories of the love that Esther had for her people and the sacrifices she made and many more. Lance began to come to church more faithfully. I began to develop my gift in ministry. We both began to work for the church. We were faithful. We considered ourselves a team. It took a lot of energy. It took a lot of time. And it took growth on both of our parts. We began to date again. We learned each other all over again. I began to glow like a newlywed. As did he.

    We went a few years getting along and with me learning to love him. I never hung his affair over his head and we never spoke it again. When I decided to move forward that meant leaving the past behind us. Soon, we returned back into a problem that he had with me. He mentioned a lot that I did not support him in his dreams. He loved sports but mainly soccer. He did not just watch it, he played them. Here he is a thirty-three year old man wanting to play soccer as if he were ten. I could not fully support that because he would always come home broken or swollen or ripped apart. What benefit was a broken boned husband to me and the children? Every time he would get hurt, he would be down for days to weeks at a time. I could not support that. That meant that I would have to play husband, wife, mother and father around our home. It was exhausting. I was still doing a lot of the work in and around the house so a lot of the burden was on me. Supporting the household while he would be down, added to my stress level. Therefore, I did not support him in that area. I realized that I was wrong. I felt that I was right, but apparently not supporting my husband in any task that he wanted to do that was not illegal or causing harm to anyone was wrong.

    Lance became very bitter towards me and began to build animosity towards me regarding the fact that I made him stop playing. He complained about gaining weight because he was not as active. He complained about not having a life because he had to stop school. Mainly, he complained to me often about how I did not support him. This was something that was dear to him and I did not have his back. Lance and I fought often about this. I should have been there for him more in this area. When I wanted something, he would support me. When I wanted to start my own business in 2007, he gave me his blessing. I did not return this favor to him regarding his sports playing because I felt that it was detrimental to our family. I felt that he was no good to our family sick and hurt all the time. No matter my feelings, I should have supported him more. It was a lesson learned but it was one that I would never live down.

Soon, our marriage began to take another turn for the worse. Our rededication and marital bliss only lasted a few years. I realized that I had stopped doing the things I used to do before I got married. I'd stopped reading, I'd stopped exercising, and I'd stopped hanging out with my friends. I had come to the conclusion that I had completely lost myself in this marriage. I was so busy trying to please him and do what he wanted me to do and try to play "good little wifee" that I lost myself. I did not even know who I was. When people would ask me what I liked to do for fun or enjoyment, my response was "I love to cook and clean and take care of my family." It took years for me to understand that that response never answered the question. Cooking and cleaning and taking care of my family was not something I enjoyed for me. It was something I enjoyed for them. I loved serving them. I loved serving my husband. I loved making him feel like a king in his house even at our worst times. However, I did not have anything I enjoyed for myself. I was so wrapped up in taking care of them that at times, all of my conversations would be about the children and how well they were doing and how much they are growing. At first, it was difficult for me to leave them at home alone with Lance because he was not that well prepared to handle the two of them alone. One day a friend of mine told me to just leave the kids there with Lance. He was a grown man and he could figure it out. I took her advice. I decided to get more involved with things outside of home and church. He got me a membership to the gym so I was there trying to lose weight three days out of the week. I later started a book club and began to lead that. Eventually, the roles were almost reversed. It was my turn to live a little. He stayed home with the children. He bathed them, fed them and got them ready for bed. I would still have to perform all of the cooking and cleaning. Thus the reason I stated "almost reversed". I still cared for my household. I still did my duties as a mother. However, when the time came for me get out of the house, I did not hesitate. It was not because I did not want to be there, but it was because I was just getting to know myself.

We began fighting a lot more. I knew that he resented me for now living my life and doing what I wanted to do and he was stuck home with the kids. He would call me repeatedly asking me when I was going to be arriving home. He would ask me to miss my scheduled appointments so that I could be at home with him and the children. When I would return home, it was a fight. I wanted to live a little. By this time, I had been married for about several years and I had just begun to live. I was not out partying and doing drugs or anything. I was just trying to find myself. He needed me and I was so far into trying to find out who I was that I became preoccupied with myself. I was into the things I wanted to be into. The way I saw it, as long as the children were safe and well taken care of, then it was not that imperative for me to be home.

Summer of 2010, the feelings that I had that something was wrong again could no longer be ignored. The same feeling that I felt back in 2006, I was feeling for months. I ignored them. I did not entertain the thoughts because I thought I was just looking for something to be wrong. At times, he would get late night text messages and phone calls. I would always convince myself that they were all business related. Even though we had our past issues, I still would not travel through his phone. Honestly, I did not want to deal with that hurt again. Until one late night, Father's Day of 2010, I sat down to use my laptop while everyone was asleep. I attempted to log in to a social media account when his email was up to log into his account. I took a deep breath and hit enter. I search through his friends to see if the person from his past was listed. It was not like I would know her face anyway. I was just curious. I begin to go to his messages and there it was. It was right there in black and white; numerous of conversations to numerous women.

When I read some of them, I was mortified. Some of the messages to these women were so disturbing that I had to walk away from the computer and cry. When I returned, I re-read them. I read them all. They included conversations from offering his phone number to offering physical favors. The messages were clear evidence of extramarital affairs. Some of the messages were to women that did not even live in the same city as us. I turned around from the computer desk that was located in our bedroom and stared at him. I was nauseated. Sickened. I would turn to read the messages and then I would turn back to simply just stare at him. As I sat in amazement, I was thinking "what am I going to do about this?"

I sat there and immediately my feelings went from hurt to anger. In a matter of minutes, I went through the feelings of loving him to disliking him. I disliked his behavior. I disliked his respect for our marriage. All the while I was at church for bible study, praise team rehearsal, the gym and book club meetings he was home on the computer doing only God knows what. I knew that I was not the best wife. I knew that I had some faults of my own. At this time the only thing I could think of was "am I that bad of a wife that this has to happen to me multiple times?" Over and over I thought about what I did to deserve this.

Originally, I decided that I was going to keep this information to myself again. After the next day of re-reading this information, I decided against that. That next day, I informed him of what I knew. Of course we had a huge falling out. I reminded him of the shame I faced the first time this came out. The people at the church knew about his affair. My friends knew as well. I had a friend that worked as a nurse at my doctor's office. She knew because I went to get tested. That had to be the most embarrassing trip to the doctor's office I had ever encountered. He was very defensive. He began to shout at me and yell because he felt I once again invaded his privacy. I decided once and for all I was done with this marriage.

Lance thought it would be good for us to go back to counseling. I declined. I did not want to go through the humiliation again. I thought after 6 years of being married, we would know how to handle this situation. I did not want to keep running to our pastor after every fight we had. I thought it was ridiculous. Granted, our pastor was there to help out and he did not recommend divorce. In fact, to our pastor, it should have not been an option. By that time, I could have cared less what the pastor, the pope or the president of the U.S.A. could have said about my marriage. I was done!

After much thought processing, I decided to stay. Deep inside, I did not want to lose our family. I wanted my children to have a father. The fear of being a single mother once again haunted me. After a few months, I grew bitter. I could not stand to be around him. I couldn't stand to smell him let alone the very sight of him. I would still complete all my duties as his wife. I did not deny him sex as his wife. We had enough issues. However, I never initiated it. I could not get pass the bitterness.

I fought to stay in the marriage. I fought really hard. It was agonizing. There were times where I would stay at the church much longer than I needed to in lieu of going home. I would ask Delicia, a young lady at the church that grew to become a baby sister of mine, to go out to eat and we would sit and talk. I would, at times, park my car in the parking lot of the grocery store nearby and wait. I would wait until I knew he was asleep and then I would go home. There were other times when I would arrive at our home and sit in the car in the garage and wait. I would just sit there. I cringed at the thought of going inside because it meant that I would have to greet him with a kiss that I knew would be fabricated.

    I was laid off of my job in September 2010; not many months after finding out this information regarding the multiple affairs. I was given a severance package. I filed for unemployment and I became a stay at home wife and mother. I was determined to make this marriage work, so I put on my big girl clothes and fought through it. Surely it would not be intelligent to leave him at this point. I wanted to continue to work on the company I started in 2007. What a perfect opportunity to be at home with my children and accomplish my dreams as a business owner. I had to stay. I had no job. I had no money. The severance and unemployment was only going to last for so long, therefore, I stayed. I convinced myself that I would fix the marriage and just go on. When that did not work, I convinced myself to stay for the children. They needed a father. They needed the man that has been taking care of them to continue to do just that in the household. We went on a family vacation. We continued to go to church together. We continued to support our children in sports. We put on the happy family faces and pretended that everything was perfect. We pretended that we had it under control even though we didn't. Everything was not perfect. Everything was not under control. It most certainly was not to me. I was sitting with Mount Vesuvius on the inside of me and it was waiting to erupt.

Things got worst. I was on an emotional roller coaster. There were times I wanted to stay and there were times I would tell him I was leaving. Lance would beg me to stay with him. He brought me gifts, played music for me and would begin to try to do more around the house. By this time, it was too late. I was already emotionally withdrawn. I would not be moved by his acts. I was still coming home when I wanted to and would not report where I was. I no longer had the respect for him that I repeated in my marital vows. I would disrespect him in front of others by not acknowledging him most of the time. Once we got home from church and he sat me down to talk to me. He told me that when we were at church he was talking and I cut him off and took over the conversation. He stated that he felt that I did not want him to have any friends nor communicate with others. It seemed to me that he had enough conversation with others. However, I was wrong in my actions. I was wrong to disrespect him that way.

I was so hurt that eventually I turned mad. Bitterness turned into a disease. I despised him for what he did. I despised myself as well. I wanted him to feel what I felt. I wanted him to hurt and be messed up emotionally too. This disease began to cost me a lot more than just my relationship with Lance. People started to notice I was not regular. I was a part of a little crew that attended the gym together. They began to ask me what was going on with me. I began to withdraw myself from them. I was in unpleasant moods often. Sometimes I would catch myself drifting off in the middle of a conversation. The more I tried to hold in my hurt and anger regarding my marriage, the more others saw the seepage take place. Indeed it was seepage. I was holding in some yucky emotions and I could not do anything about it. I held in the fact that I really wanted to leave him. I wanted to scream and yell at him. I wanted to punch him…again. I wanted to run away and leave everything. Things were so intense that I wanted to leave my children behind. But that did not last too long, I love my children.

Lance was beginning to feel the fact that I no longer wanted him. I had no interest in being with him any longer. His behavior turned from trying his best with different tactics to keep me with him to actually *forcing* me to stay with him. He would often threaten to harm himself if I left him. One day I was at an event when I received a notice on my phone that stated that the main account holder, Lance, had created a service on his phone and was currently using it. It was a GPS tracker. Lance put a GPS tracker on my phone! I cannot really describe the feeling I got when I received that notice. I was furious. It was like he was so upset that the tactics were not working that he would now try to control every move I made. He began to tell me certain times I had to be home. He would question me when I would leave the house or when I would arrive to the house about my whereabouts. He then attempted to control my every move. One night I caught him searching through my phone. His excuse was that he was looking for a phone number of a mutual friend of ours. Soon after, he requested that we meet with our pastor for additional counseling sessions. Lance reported to the pastor that one day I act like I love him and the next day I act like I hate him. The pastor told him that I was on an emotional roller coaster given the situation. Lance did not want to hear that. It appeared that he wanted to hear that I was wrong for being that way. The pastor told him that he would have to soak it up when I was in the good place and still love me when I was in the bad ones.

    I was miserable. I would put the children to bed and just sit on the edge of my bed. I would turn to look at him sleeping and I would just sit and cry. If I wanted any sleep at all, I would have to cry myself to sleep. I would think to myself, "Why would God punish me like *this*?" I knew that I had not been the perfect wife, but was all this suffering necessary? My sanity was on the line here. This went on for nights, until night after night became month after month. Eventually, I was so miserable that I began to get sick. The fight to stay in the marriage and try to keep my family afloat was beginning to wear and tear on my body. I was vomiting every night. I could not hold anything down. Lance would try to console me. Even until this day, I appreciate him for that. I know it was not easy trying to assist the woman who despised the very sight of him. I began to lose weight. I was so stressed out. I could barely focus at work. I became malnourished. My co-workers and close friends began to see a change in my bubbly personality. It became dull. I was crying out for help in the inside, but I did not even know how to ask for it. I was too prideful.

Miserableness took over my spirit. Although I was still taking care of my duties as a mother and partially as a wife, the truth is, I wanted to run away. I wanted to get away from it all. I never wanted to come back. I thought it was better for me to just escape and leave everything behind. I did not run away. I stayed. I stayed in misery. I stayed in heartbreak and I stayed in bitterness. This went on for months before I wanted revenge. The misery had to go. I was a happy person and I could not be miserable for too much longer because my health was at stake, people were beginning to notice things were wrong in my happy little marriage and I did not like feeling defeated. I wanted to feel that somewhere down the line I was going to win.

From my vantage point, our marriage was destroyed. We both completely dishonored our vows to one another. I had no respect for him. I did not love him anymore and frankly, I was utterly emotional withdrawn from him. I could already barely stand the very sight of him. I did not want him touching me but I allowed it. I did not want him around me but I allowed it. I fought through every emotion I had to try to still be a wife. Being a good wife was not in question because my mental and emotional status was too far gone for that. I yet still ironed his clothes for work. I yet and still cleaned behind him. I yet and still served him his dinner and come back to collect his dishes. I yet and still greeted him with a kiss. However, I had enough of crying and being sad and miserable. I was sick of fighting to stay in this marriage. It was over for me. But because of my children and the image that I had to keep for my position in the church, the church itself and its members, I stayed. I was also very afraid of leaving. I had no idea what was going to be the outcome of our future. I stayed for everyone else but me! Soon, I took it upon myself to at least cope with it somehow. All the submitting and patience in the world was not enough to stop me from what I was about to do about it. Unfortunately, my coping mechanism was an affair.

    An old male friend reached out to me after a long period of time of not speaking or seeing each other. After he found out I married, he moved on with his life. Upon his return, we began to communicate a lot more than we should have. I began to tell him my issues in my marriage and look to him for him to comfort me. Only after a short time of reconnecting, we decided to move from phone and email conversations to seeing each other in person. I knew it was not a good idea but at that time in my marriage, I did not care. Needless to say, I had an affair with this man.

    When I left from his presence, I felt awful. I felt dreadful. I was appalled at the fact that I could do such a thing. I was horrified that I even went through with it. I thought I was big and bad and strong. I was not. I was sick for days post this deceitful action. I too betrayed my vows. I went back on my word. I was wrong. I vowed to belong to Lance and no one else. I gave my body to another man that was not my husband. I went to God and begged for repentance. Day after day and night after night, I beseeched and pleaded with God. I thought He was going to kill me. I thought God was going to take me out of this world. I just knew my time was near. I am grateful for grace and mercy from my savior. I continued my relationship with Lance as if nothing ever happened. I still knew I eventually had to pay the consequences for my actions.

I needed to escape the mental and emotional distraught I was going through. But mainly, I wanted revenge. It was not that I wanted Lance to hurt, I just wanted out of the feeling that I sacrificed so much to be with him and he completely treated me like I did not deserve to have him sacrifice for me as well. I was distraught at first, but eventually, the feeling grew to guilt. Each time after my decision to commit adultery, I was taunted with guilt. Each time I looked Lance in the face, I realized that I was just like him. I rationalized my behavior. For four consistent years I was cheated on, I was manipulated and controlled. I thought that we were getting better. But to find out the whole time we were in counseling and working on our marriage, he was still having affairs completely shattered me. So, it gave me my reason to do what I did. I figured "how important are our vows if He doesn't care about them. They are already broken now". Even though it was only for a very short time, I was just as guilty as Lance.

I did not stay in the hurt feeling too long. I became angry. The bitterness grew to another level. I felt it was mainly because of all the sacrifices I made, the fight to stay, the embarrassment and the cover up. No one knew how Lance truly was. I covered him. I made him seem like he was God's gift to me. I thought that was what a wife should have done. I thought it was my responsibility to cover his faults. That did not last long. When I would be with my friends, they could hear him yelling and screaming through the phone. When I would tell them what he said or would do, they could not believe it. His need to control me grew stronger. He would threaten to come where I was with my friends and pick me up to bring me home. He began to fight with me just to have conversation. It appeared any type of communication with me was communication. Unfortunately, it would be arguments. It seemed like we fought every day and night. Some days would be ok and others, I just wanted to ram my head into a red brick wall. It would piss him off even more when I would not entertain his arguments. He would not get physical with me by hitting me but he would get in front of me and point his fingers in my face while yelling. When I would attempt to walk away he would get angrier. Therefore, at times, I would just sit through it. Inside, I was torn. I was destroyed. Because of his need to keep me with him, his actions ended up tearing me down. The fighting and yelling for any reason at all became exhausting. I remember looking at him thinking, "This cannot be love. This is insanity."

In attempt to catch a small break from it all, I gathered a small group of friends to have a girl's weekend. I was only 15 miles from home, in a hotel room with five of my friends and only gone for one night. He refused to let me enjoy it. He called me consistently. He threatened to come and ruin my trip, and he demanded that I leave them and come home early. I did not. In fact, to be spiteful, I came home later than I even wanted to. We fought the next morning before church and he started again when we got home that afternoon. I just could not take it anymore. The word "miserable" became an understatement. It was pure agony to sit and fight for no apparent reason. For us to ignore each other, sleep in separate rooms, and put up this façade in front of others was insane. I asked him to leave the house because I no longer wanted to be with him anymore. After he put up a fight, he packed some things in a red and black duffle bag and left. He told me that he would go to his mother's house if that's what I wanted. I'll never forget the hopeless look in his eye. He kissed the children and walked out the door. About 15 minutes later, he called me to. We ended up yelling and fighting once again. While I was yelling at him, the bedroom door opened, it was him. He waltzed right back into the house and told me he was not leaving. I said, "Fine then, I will leave". I packed my suitcase and my children's things. I had had it! I was tired of the fighting. I was tired of the bitterness I felt and I was tired of staying for reasons other than just for me. I once wanted my marriage and I was willing to do any and everything to salvage it. Not this time. Lance called the pastor in frantic and informed him I was leaving the house. When the pastor asked to speak to me, I knocked the phone out of Lance's hands. I grabbed my things, grabbed the children and walked out the door. I left everything behind: My house. My furniture. My livelihood. I had no job. I had no money. I really did not even have a place to go. All I had was a broken and shattered heart and my children. It was April 10, 2011 and on that day, my world was shaken and flipped; my life changed forever.

PART II-THE RIPPING

It was my third attempt at completing my college degree. I had only been back in school for four months when I decided to leave Lance. After all it took for me to get back in school, I just knew this time was going to be the season I actually completed my dream. There were two people who fought very hard with me and motivated into going back to school, TaKeela, my cousin and Jertoria, a young lady who grew to be like a baby sister to me. These women took out the time to walk into the office with me to get me registered, they made phone calls for me and they both gave me reasons for not giving up. After I got the nerve build up, only four months after I am in school, registered with classes that I feel that I was going to give up yet again.

My goal was to separate from Lance. Things were too heated between the both of us. I loved him. I cared a great deal for him. Although I was not doing everything the right way, deep inside, I wanted our marriage to work. I ended the short affair I was having. I was too distraught to make anything more complicated than what I was. I did not leave Lance on account of my affair. To me, I knew it was wrong. Yet it was a coping mechanism to deal with what I dealt with. I spent nights crying out to God for answers. Those nights turned into weeks, and the weeks turned into months. I wanted God to see how miserable I was. I knew I had messed up and I knew I was messed up. I often thought why God would help me knowing that I was just as wrong as Lance. I needed him to give me answers. I needed to know what move to make. The last thing I wanted to do was move and not be in the will of God for my life. Many people have their own interpretation, views and opinions when it comes to marriage, separation and divorce. The truth is, the decision is between God and that person according to His word.

When I left, I took some clothes and I went to my Godparents house. Not wanting me and my children to be on the street, they were kind enough to open up their home to me. I cried every day and all night. At times, I thought I had no clue what I was doing. At other times, I felt it was the right thing to do. I thought maybe we would just have some time a part until we could sort through our issues. Things began to become realistic soon. I had to drive my children to the bus stop every morning. My Godparents lived in another town north of us and it took about 30-40 minutes in commute to reach my house from theirs. I had a SUV at the time. I suffered. I hardly had any money and the gas from that commute was a pain. I would drop them off to the bus stop, chance seeing Lance and fighting with him. Then I would go to school and attempt to focus, and then stay on that side of town until the children were out of school!

For the very life of me, I could not understand how he could be ok with the fact that his family was living with another family. Although it was my decision to leave because he would not, I still did not understand it. He would send flowers to their house for me and continue to push the fact that he wanted us together.

I stayed with my Godparents for a week before Lance called me and agreed to leave the house. I moved back to my house along with my children. Lance was not at the house when I arrived. He moved in with his mother. Another reality set in: I was alone. I was in this huge house, huge bed, alone. I had no one to lay my head on. I had no one to talk to about how my day went. I began to realize that this was exactly what I thought it was going to be. I did not want to go through this. Even though things were bad between us, I hated every second that he was not lying in bed with me. After being married for so long, it was only natural that I become accustom to sleeping beside him. The pain began to set in. I was not happy at all that this was happening. Although I made the decision to not be with him anymore, we were still married.

This was the first time, even after all of the nonsense we had been through before, that we had been apart. It literally felt like a ripping. Every second that he was away from me, it felt like my arm was detaching from my body. If I could really describe how it felt, it felt like little by little, different parts of my body were ripping from my torso. I could literally feel us ripping apart from each other. Our spirits began to separate. We were one at one time, now, we were two.

The ripping effect became more intense after a while. More and more I would often question whether I made the right decision to leave. I did not want to disappoint others, mainly God. The more and more I stayed away from him, the more I would feel pain. Confusion began to set in as I wondered if this was "good" pain, or was it "bad" pain? I wondered if I was doing the right thing the wrong way or the wrong thing in general. When Lance did not get what he wanted, which was to have us back together, he would "act out". There were countless times that Lance would attempt to manipulate me by threatening to harm himself or threatening to take away my daughter. He attempted to hurt me with words as well as actions. This would be the time I learned the lesson "hurt people hurt people".

EXHALE MOMENT! TAKE A MOMENT AND RELEASE!!!

THE KNOCKOUT

Around this time, I was still in school. I would go to school sad every time I went. Each day I went, I thought I would gain more hope about my future. But I did not. I was reminded that I had no money to pay for school because I had no job. I received letters from the school stating that I owed them money. I was not receiving any financial help outside of a scholarship that only covered the base of my tuition. I had to pay for books out of pocket. The only thing I had in my pockets was lent and cotton. The school did not accept that for payment.

It was not long before the financial burden of being a single struggling mother hit home. I could barely feed me or my children. There were times when I had to feed my children dinner and I would not eat anything at all. I was going to school smiling and doing my work, but I was so broken inside. My mind was constantly on what I was going to do. I had no clue. I had no plan. I received my first "C" that semester. I barely passed the class because I could not stay focused long enough to study the material for the class. I was devastated. This was my third attempt at college and I needed my dreams to come true. Therefore, the ambition and drive that I exuded came from pure determination.

My life was flipped upside down. Soon, people at the church began to ask me if everything was ok. The truth is they knew that it was not. The people at the church saw me cry every time I entered the church. I removed my wedding band so I was certain that they saw that too. Lance and I drove separate cars to church as well. The embarrassment that came along with that was almost unbearable. However, I kept in mind that this was my decision and boy, was I paying for it.

Lance's attitude would shift upon my decision to not allow him back at the house. He would go from extremely distraught which included him crying and pleading with me to exceptionally angry which included nasty comments to me and hateful phone voicemails. He would go from one tactic of trying to get me back to another tactic of showing me that he could survive without me and I was going to regret leaving him. He would say the most awful things you would want to hear. They would hurt me to my soul. I would hang up the phone and go in the restroom to hide from my children, close the door and boo-hoo cry like a baby. I could not believe that He was doing and saying the things that he did. The way I saw it, he should have just let it be. He should have just let us separate. If He would have just gave me some space, maybe we could have reconciled. We could have attempted to work it out. With everything that He was doing and saying, he was making it really hard for me to want to work anything out with him.

About three weeks after He left the house and I came back, Lance asked me at church if we could speak. He stated to me that he wanted to have an adult conversation with me. He appeared very calm and sincere so I agreed. I let my children go with a sitter and after church he followed me to the house we purchased together. When we got to the house, I welcomed him in through the front door. In he walks with that same red and black duffle bag that he packed when I first asked him to leave. To my surprise, he walked right by with a grin on his face that I would never forget. I begin to question what was going on. He waltzed by the kitchen, through the living room and into our bedroom. He plopped his bag on the bed and told me to sit down. I continued to stay standing. After inquiring what he was doing, Lance informed me that he had spoken to our pastor and after some thought, he was returning home with or without my blessings. Imagine the shock that was upon my face. He gave me this whole spill about how it was his house and either I could stay in another room or I could leave the house. He then took away my choice and told me to get out of his house. He informed me that he was paying the bills, his name was on the house and that he was not leaving anymore. He sounded very authoritative and serious. I could not do anything but then take his advice and sit upon shock. He gave me this speech about how wrong I was for putting him out of *his* house and making him feel like less of a man. While he proceeded to give me his speech, he asked me for my keys. Then, he began to search my things for my keys. I told him that I was not leaving. After he took my keys to the house, His response was, "this is *my* house!" I did not want to leave my house. I put in the time and effort to take care of that house. It was warmth in it because of me. It was painted because of me. It was well kept because of me. There was no way I was leaving my house.

Soon after, he left out of the room smiling. It was if something had come over him. As I sat on the edge of the bed, I could not stop the tears from coming. I was full of too many emotions to name: anger, hurt and embarrassment. I could not understand if I was crying because of these emotions or because of shock. I stayed on the edge of the bed and then I heard him on the phone. It appeared he called one of his friends. He began to utter some words like this: "hey man, why don't you and a few of yall come over tonight. Yeah, I'm single now, so let's party!" Then afterwards, I turned my head to the left of me to see him plug his phone into the stereo system. He began to play the song *I Smile* by Kirk Franklin and started dancing around the living room. Instantly, I felt my insides burning. For years, I hated that song. My hands began to tremble; tears stopped flowing from my eyes. I was furious. I was beyond livid. How could a man put his wife and children out on the street? I know that I had not been the best, that was all that I was thinking, but I did not deserve to be put out of my house. I then grabbed a few items and walked towards the door. He ran after me and stopped in the kitchen. He grabbed me by both my arms. He looked me in the eye and pleaded with me not to leave. He began to tell me that I could stay in the other room so that we both could continue to live in the house. He was totally confusing. I was beginning to see his manipulation seep out of his pores. However, by this time, I was so repulsed and fuming that I did not digest what he was saying.

After some words exchanging, he began to force himself on me. He smashed his lips against mine and attempted to kiss me long and hard. With all force that I had in me, I pushed him off me and he fell onto the kitchen floor. I ran out of house, jumped into my SUV and left the house that I had built with him all of four years. I attempted to push the garage door button but realized that he had removed it from my vehicle.

Driving away from the house, I broke down. I had to pull over as soon as I got out of the subdivision because I could not see from all the tears that were draining from my eyes. My hands were still quivering. My heart was beating fast. I just placed my face in both hands and let it out. I screamed to the top of my lungs, "WHAT IS GOING ON WITH MY LIFE?!" I was completely unhappy. I picked up the phone and called a friend of mine who was a realtor. I began to ask him about any houses to rent. He could hear my voice trembling. As I told him some of the things that were going on, he began to sympathize with me. I then called my Godmother and asked her for permission to return back to her house. With open arms and an open generous heart, both my godparents agreed to let me and the children once again return to their home.

The following week, I put on my big girl boots and went on a hunt. I went apartment and house shopping. I was grateful for my godparents for opening up their home to me and my children. However, I was not going to take advantage of their generosity. I needed to be on my own. I could never depend on people too long before my independence in me would rise up. Looking for a place to stay became exhausting. I was still in school, I still had to travel back and forth with my children to take them to school and I still had the financial burden on me.

One day I went to go pick up the children from Lance at the house. He would have his moments of being nice and trying to comfort me. I cried out to God for answers. I cried to God for comfort. I began to worship God right there on the sofa until I fell asleep. I needed God to bring me out of this. I did not understand what was going on with me emotionally, so I turned to the only help I knew: God. A few weeks later, Lance asked me once again to come back to the house for good and that he would leave. I returned back to my home but I still continued to look for places in case he pulled another "this is my house" stunt.

My emotions began to take complete control of my life. I did not rely on the comfort of others, I could hardly pray and my relationships with others began to go downstream. Soon, people began to treat me differently. Some of the members from the church would call me and try to pray me back with my husband. They would say things like, "Divorce is not of God and you need to think about what you are doing". Soon, the relationship with my leaders began to become unstable. I understood that everyone wanted our marriage to work. But to me, I was treated like an outcast because of the stories Lance was going around telling people. He would talk to my parents often. He would try to convince them to talk to me and make me realize that we needed to reconcile and leaving him was a mistake. It seemed like everyone had their hand in the matter of our separation and actually believe the things he was saying. I was told the lies that Lance had been telling mutual friends and my family. Some of the lies were so out of my character that it amused me how those same people who knew me for years, some even my whole life, had believed them. It was not long before proof that people were believing him would start to become noticeable to me. People at the church, even the leaders, would walk by me and not speak. It seemed as if their attitude towards me changed. Eventually, I was told that I could not operate in my duties at the church. I was told to my face that I had become bitter and arrogant. This hurt, but I muscled through it all. I attended church with a smile. My character had been attacked. I was humiliated often at church because of actions by Lance to start disagreements in public places such as church. Yet, I still attempted to hold it together.

The real relationship shaker was when my parents began to treat me different. Lance went to the hospital for passing out at work. I found out through a mutual friend. When I called to find out what was going on, Lance did not want to give me information about where he was or what happened. After I gathered information from my parents and other friends that he gave this information to, I went to visit him. He would not talk to me nor tell me what happened therefore, after visiting for all of ten minutes, I left. I did not feel bad or remorseful. In fact, I went to the movies with my close friends for some pick-me-ups. My mother called me that night after she was informed about it from Lance. She was very upset with me and she began to yell. She told me that she did not understand how I could be at the movies having fun while my husband was in the hospital. Then she disconnected the phone call and when I tried returning the call, she would not pick up. The next day, I called my mother and stepfather numerous times. I was so hurt that they would not answer my calls. I was feeling so betrayed. First, some of my church family turns their back on me and now my parents?! I was outraged. Eventually, my parents answered the phone. I cried to my mother informing her how I felt. I informed her that I felt they were taking his side only by the lies and manipulation he was putting forth. I felt that they did not hear me at all and was only listening to him. Finally, I told my mother these few words, "watch His actions. See if they align with what he says to you. All you have to do is see for yourself."

My desire was not to harm Lance with lies, but mainly the truth of our situation. Even after all of the things he did through our marriage and throughout the separation, I still did not show or tell others what was really going on. I still felt the need to hide him. Delicia would often ask me, "Why are you still taking up for him? Why won't you just be honest and tell everyone what a liar He really is? Why won't you expose him?" He was still my husband. I had not realized how much I had been covering up for him. I did not want people to know I had decided to stay with such a monster because honestly, he was not all that bad. At least, that is what I would tell others. If he wasn't all that bad, why was I feeling the way I was? Why was I the one being put out of our house with my two small children? Why was I being punished by our friends and fellow church members? Why was I being reprimanded by my pastor and striped from my responsibilities?

The pain did not go away because the actions of Lance and others did not go away. I prayed and asked God to show me who I was, show me who I had become. He did, God showed me in a dream that I was bitter because I was being treated so unfairly but I was not arrogant. I was only trying to save others by hiding their faults. But God also showed me that's his job, not mine. I asked God to help me with the pain. That prayer seemed to me like it went into the folder titled "unanswered". The pain continued when some people would call me and ask if I was ok, others would not even bother to pick up the phone. Regardless what people's thoughts and values were about divorce and separation, I did not deserve such horrible treatment. I called another person who I knew had a hard time and was reprimanded for deciding to leave her husband. I apologized to her. She had no clue what I was apologizing for. I told her what I was going through and informed her that I did not realize the effect separation has on a person and that I was sorry for not supporting her decision as much as I could have.

I soon had to separate myself. The pain was increasing by the minute. I was already having a rough time with Lance alone, but the treatment I was receiving from those that said they loved me and who I had invested time and care in became unbearable. I took a leave of absence from the church for a few weeks. During this time, I attended another church in search for healing and restoration. It helped but it didn't do me any justice because during this time, I did not receive any concern from my pastor but I received concern and care from a few fellow church members. Imagine investing your time, energy, personal assets and money into a ministry and as soon as you go through a traumatic experience in your life and you get no assistance from the place that people are instructed and pleaded with to go get assistance from. I had never felt so alone in my life. Not only was I facing divorce from my husband but I also had to face the reality that some people only want what you have to offer and when they can't receive that, they are done with you. I felt tossed aside. Sure, I received phone calls from some friends and family. Some of them were to just be plain ole' nosey yet only a few showed genuine concern. So, after a few weeks of taking a leave of absence, I returned to my church. I only stayed for two more weeks before I made the final decision to leave for good.

People began to see the real Lance come out months after our separation. A good friend of mine would ask me why I would hide him so much, but I always said time will tell. My mom and stepdad soon after our conversation came around to know the truth. My mother called me and apologized to me for what appeared as though she was taking Lance's side. She explained to me that she only wanted the best for me and that she thought that that meant Lance and I staying married. She told me that she began to watch his actions as I instructed her to and she began to see him for who he really was. In fact, a lot of others begin to see the same thing. Lance began to do some of the awful things to me. Some of the awful things included getting into another relationship only three months after our separation. He canceled my car insurance policy without my knowledge. He would speak so nasty to me that I thought I was speaking to another person. But it was like as soon as he would realize what he had done, he would be so sad and apologize. I could never understand it. I believe the most hurtful thing he could do out of all of the things he had done was when he disowned my son. All of these years, he had taken offense to people calling my son his stepson and all the time he cherished him as his son, he told me one day that he was not his son and that he did not have to care for him any longer. He was not going to pay child support or finance him at all any further. Initially when the break up first happened, he would get both of the children every weekend. This only lasted about six months. My mother went ballistic when she found out. She saw him differently after we all found out about his relationship with another woman and brought her to the church we used to attend together. However, she lost all respect for him when he did not want to care for Jaden any longer. My mother is a lunatic when it comes to her grandchildren. Although she forgives him, she never spoke to him again.

    I was hit with a double whammy: separation from my husband and then separation from my church family. No one in this world should have to go through such agony. I felt as if my life was over. I had to face the embarrassment and disappointment of those that saw me as a leader. I had to face that same disappointment from the children that attended the church that looked up to me and my marriage. I had to face the fact of how I was perceived! How did they view me now? How did anyone view me? A failure? Well, that is what I went with. I saw myself as a failure. I should have just suffered through my rough times with Lance. I should have done more work at the church. I should have done more for my pastor and his family. Maybe I should have told the truth about him to the world. Maybe I should have thrown him under the bus as he did me although it was not my character. When those people who would talk about how bad of a person I was for leaving my husband and my church, maybe I should have retaliated. At that time, if anyone would have asked me if I wanted to do this all over again, I would have said "no". I would have just suffered through my marriage to avoid this discomfort. I experienced every emotion in the book following these two traumatic experiences: divorce from my husband and divorce from the church in which I was deeply involved. However, it was not over, God was not through taking me through the fire. As if I needed anymore lighter fluid added to this fire, on February 11, 2012, only days after visiting with her, my maternal Grandmother passed on from this earth to be with the Lord.

THE TURMOIL

My grandmother was one of the reasons I became a minister. She herself was a preacher and let me tell you, she could pray a house down. On February 7th, I went to visit her in the hospital. She had a minor heart attack while receiving dialysis. On that day I went to visit her, I was dressed business casual as I had to meet with Lance for mediation for our divorce. When I went to see her, she was so full of life. She made me laugh and I made her laugh as well. One thing she kept telling me was how pretty I looked. When I first walked in she said to me, "Oh Trenda, you look so pretty today!" I replied, "Today?! What about all the other days?" We shared a laugh. Upon my departure from my grandmother which was the last time I heard her sweet voice, she said to me again, "Trenda, you are so pretty!" I said, "You are too, grandma!"

She said, "Oh no, honey, that's the God you see in me!" Those words would stick with me through the worst and lowest part of my life.

Lance offered me his condolences but he did not show up at any of the services for my grandmother. I thought that was wrong for him to not show his face and support my family because they had been there for him in his time of loss but I did not show much concern about it. I believe I was so focused on the loss that I did not pay much attention to his actions.

When you lose someone that meant so much to you and your family, it seems unreal. My best friend Keva told me, "Although it is extremely hard to do this, you must celebrate her life instead of moping in her death. But, I felt as broken as broken could get. People came to visit our family. They brought food and laughter. While others were enjoying family time and hugs, I was sinking deeper and deeper into a dark hole. The night my grandmother passed away, Delicia came home with me. I don't remember saying too much to her. I was down and beyond sad. I proceeded to take a shower. While showering all I remember was thinking about how difficult my life was at that very moment. I thought about the hardships I was facing. I had no hope. I knew that everything was downhill from this point on. All I saw was darkness. I saw no light. Even though Delicia was talking, all I could hear was mumbling.

I must have been in the shower to long because Delicia came to see what was going on. As soon as she opened the door to the shower, I collapsed in her arms. My body went limp. Everything after that was a blur.

For the next few weeks, I stayed in bed. I only went to class when I had to go and I returned back home. I did not want to see anyone. I did not want to talk to anyone. All I wanted to do was sleep. Life's issues were becoming too much for me. I was grieving three things at one time: two divorces and a death of a loved one. With all of that going on, I did not even want to bathe. I could barely take care of my children. There were many nights they ate cereal for dinner. Now, that was heaven for them, but for me it spoke about my parenting. I felt like a horrible mother because I could barely care for them. Eventually, I got out of bed and begin to paint the house.

I could barely support myself financially let alone two kids. I was still in school full time and wanted my business to flourish. Whatever I could put my hands on that made money legally, I did it. I began to hustle and try to promote my company to gain more clientele. I started working part time for a cosmetic company to bring some funds in, I cooked weekly meals for families and I delivered them and I even cleaned houses for people. I worked my butt off! I had to do what I had to do to make ends meet for my family. This experience only made me question myself. "Did I do the right thing?" "Should I have left him?" "Was I making a mistake?"

While all of these tragic events happening, I needed an outlet. I was about to lose it. My spiritual life began to decrease. I felt like God had left me alone to fend for myself. I felt that He put me through this but for what, I was unclear. I began to isolate myself even more. Sometimes I wouldn't pick up the phone from my close friends. Keva, Delicia, Richard and Valerie would call me over and over and I would just stare at the phone. I knew they wanted me to be happy again. But I did not have it in me. Sometimes they would just pop up at my house and take me out somewhere.

Soon I turned to an outlet that almost got me hooked. I was on the verge of a major addiction. I began to drink alcohol. I drank every night for almost a year. Sometimes I would drink until I fell asleep. Only my close friends knew it was getting as bad as it was because I started purchasing the small bottles that you can carry around with you like the ones they give out at the airport. They messed up when they made those. I would carry them with me anytime we went somewhere. Then I would try to pull my friends in to drink with me. I guess I didn't want to miserable by myself. Night after night, I would pour myself a "night cap". At first, I started drinking because I knew it would help me sleep. Since I was having such a hard time falling asleep at night, I would use that to help me sleep. Then, I realized that when I was drinking, I did not think about the separation. I was always anxious, so the drink would help me relax. At least, that is what I told myself.

I was so ashamed of myself. I was a licensed minister, mother, and a student trying to succeed in life but most importantly I was supposed to be a Christian; a person who believed in Jesus Christ and served him as my Master. I was supposed to believe that *He* would take care of my every need and come to my rescue. Well, the truth was He did not come when I thought He should. I prayed all the time for God to help me in this divorce. I would cry myself to sleep at night because of the load of hurt, disappointment and shame I was carrying, not to mention guilt. It was not until I really learned what depression was until I figured out and came to the conclusion that I was depressed. As a Christian, we are taught that we are "too blessed to be stressed" and we do not believe in depression. Well, the truth is, it is real. Depression is real and it can happen to anyone who claims to be a human being.

In depression, you become isolated. I just wanted to be alone. I did not want anyone around me. I did not want to talk much to people and in fact, I did not want to meet any new people. By this time I started my core classes in my program at school. The people were so giddy and happy. I remember the first day of my *Introduction to Group Therapy* class. I sat there as the teacher explained that we would leave this class with friends and future colleagues. I rolled my eyes so hard I could feel a nerve pop! I was just thinking "just give me my syllabus and let me do my work so I can go home, get my drink and go to sleep. One of the ladies in the class came up to me and said that we were going to be friends; once again, I rolled my eyes. I used to be the type that introduced myself with a smile and wanted everyone to be my friend, at this point, I just wanted to do the basics: hello and goodbye. On the contrary, I hated sleeping alone. There were times I would call one of my close friends over to come stay over with me. I spent the last seven years in the bed with someone so sleeping alone was an adjustment. Even until this day, I still have a hard time adjusting.

At times, I would have spurts of anger. I was angry at my former pastor, I was angry at God and I was angry at Lance. I was angry at my former pastor for taking away my responsibilities. I mean, ministry was all I had that was valuable to me outside of my business. I think I was more upset that He took my responsibilities away and not Lance's. Lance was still able to operate in the church and not me. So, I was angry. I was angry at God because I felt abandoned. I was still praying, still thanking him for life, health and strength but yet, it did not appear to me that He was acting on my behalf. I felt like Lance was getting all the glory and attention. I felt that I was not God's favorite person at that time. I was angry at Lance because I would think about all the good I did for him. I would think about all the times I sacrificed for him and all of the current things he was doing and saying to me. I went to drop off my daughter to him one afternoon and he just had this ridiculous smirk on his face. It was like a slap in my face. I was in my SUV and his car was parked across the driveway from where I parked. When I got ready to leave, I turned over the ignition to my SUV and stared at the new car he purchased. I pushed the gas pedal to rev the ignition up. Tears formulated in my eyes as I wanted to put my car in drive and run my SUV slap into his brand new vehicle. I was raging with anger! Every fiber, every cell and every ounce of energy I had was getting ready for this outburst of rage. I soon pulled the gear shift down to neutral. I had both hands on the steering wheel. I was contemplating on if I should drive my truck into the back of his car and not stop until the car ran into the apartment building. I looked over and with blurry vision, I saw my son in the passenger seat. I then stared at him because it was obvious that I needed to be brought back to reality. I pulled the gear shift down one more gear to Drive and drove off out of the parking lot. My son asked me what was wrong but I just gave him some excuse because I did not want him to know the truth. I needed an outlet for my anger. Therefore, I began to go to the gun range. It may not have been the best thing to do to have a gun in my hand while depressed *and* angry, but it helped a lot! It was either I go and put some bullet holes in a piece of paper or I use my vehicle as a weapon. I chose to stay out of jail so I went to the range.

I was so depressed and things were so bad for me that I could literally feel my head about to explode. My mom called me one day and asked me if I was prepared for an event our family had to attend. I remember being so confused. I asked her "when is it, again?"

She said, "Trenda, it's in two weeks!"

I said to her calmly, "Mother, I am just trying to make it until 8pm tonight. If I make it to 8pm tonight, I can then think about making it to 10pm. Please do not ask me about something two weeks from now when it takes every bit of energy in me just to make it hour by hour."

I felt that something was taking over my mind. It was so dark. All I saw was darkness. I could not see pass the moment I was in. It was like walking through a dark alley with no flashlight, no street lights, and with a blindfold on. Every feeling there is to feel, I felt it. I felt sadness, anger, frustration, guilty, disappointed, unloved, regret, hate, powerless, manipulated, and resentful and the list goes on.

I grew hate in my heart. I hated Lance. I hated him for what he was putting me through and what he had done. The very sound of his name made my stomach turn. I hated myself. I hated the choices I made. I was never taught to hate. I never experienced hate in my heart. When it came upon me, I did not know how to handle it. I needed healing. I knew it.

I had bad thoughts. I had thoughts that we are taught Christians do not have. There were times I would fall asleep with both of my hands wrapped around my head and just pray. One night, I was in my room with the door locked after feeding the children dinner. My mind was racing. I was fighting fixing myself a drink. Thoughts of my grandmother passing, both divorces, I was completely losing it. I paced the floor back and forth. Back and forth I walked from one side of the room to the other. Finally, the thoughts I had been fighting overwhelmed me. Suicide. I wanted to leave this earth for the simple fact of escaping this pain. The pain, the hurt and the anger was too much to bear. I was exhausted. I was tired of hustling trying to make ends meet, tired of school, tired of the kids bickering, tired of Lance still doing selfish tactics to get under my skin, I was just tired! Mostly, I was tired of fighting. I had no more energy left in me to fight this agony. I had no more ambition in me to make it to the next day. I found a piece of paper that was on my desk. I was crying hysterically. I wanted to write down something. I just did not know what to write. I did not even have a plan to commit suicide. I just wanted it all to end. My hand was shaking. The tears eventually rolled on to the empty sheet of paper. As I attempted to write something, there was a knock on my bedroom door.

GETTING TO THE LIGHT

When I opened my bedroom door, I saw my children's faces. They saved my life. They reminded me that they needed me. That sound of that knock was, at that time, the best sound in the world. God sent them right on time. Before I opened the door, I yelled and told the kids to hold on a second. I ran to the restroom to wash my face. When I got to the door, the kids both gave me this huge hug and told me they loved me.

Throughout this whole process, I never cried in front of my children. I did not want them to see how much pain I was in. They are both very caring and compassionate kids, so I knew if I cried and showed them how I was feeling, they would pick up on it. They often asked me if I was ok. The truth is, no matter how much I tried to hide it I knew they picked up on my sorrow anyway.

A few years before all of this happened a woman by the name of Bishop RaVonda Nesbitt came to visit our church. From the time we met, I knew she would be a significant part of my life. I asked her to be my spiritual mentor. She agreed and from that moment on she was there for me. I called her almost every single day throughout this process. At times, I did not want to hear anything she had to say. I knew she was going to want to pray and to be honest I wouldn't be in the mood. No matter how much I tried to deny her help and support, she kept calling me. She kept sending me text messages and encouraging me. She would call me and just tell me she loved me. The times I wouldn't answer the phone, she would leave a voicemail forcing me to contact her. "My Pumpkin, I know you see me calling you, you better call me back," she would say in the sweetest voice. She never judged me nor did she make light of my situation. I entrusted her with confidential information and she ensured me that she would be there for me.

I cried a lot. At night, I would have to cry myself to sleep. Crying was my release. It helped me release all of the hurt, the pain and the anger. There was no restrictions on where I would cry. Sometimes, I would cry as soon as I walked into a church or someone said something to me that encouraged me. I was on the phone with my Godfather Rod one day and all he did was tell me how proud he was of me and I broke down. I think he did too! My father would call and check on me, he always made me cry because he would speak so well of me and pour good things into me. The reason why that made such a difference was because my father was not the mushy type. Years ago I would have to pull his ear and yank his arm behind his back just to get him to say "I love you". However, during this process, he was very encouraging. He would often tell me the same thing over and over again, "Trenda, just be faithful to God. Stay faithful to him, fall in place and He will make you ruler over much".

I was sick of being in the condition I was in. As I cried, I finally told God I needed His help. I cried out to God so loud and so hard, that I thought I was going to wake the neighborhood. I realized that I had just stopped. I stopped at life. I had no hope. Well, that time was over. Although all of my tears I considered liquid prayers, it was time to fight and not cry.

The very next Sunday after I left my previous church, I went to visit The Ekklesia Church. The pastor there, Major C. Jones II, used to be one of the ministers to the "mother" church I used to attend, so I was fairly comfortable with him. When I walked into the church, I immediately begin to cry. So many of the people I used to fellowship with were members as well. They came over and hugged me with such a warm embrace. I was an emotional wreck. The fact that I was there on a Sunday morning was a clear giveaway to those who knew I held a heavy position at my previous church. I called Pastor Major and his wife the next night. I only told them basic information that I felt they needed to know. I gave them no details. I just wanted him to know that I would be fellowshipping with them and their ministry for a little while.

Sunday after Sunday, I allowed him to pray for me. I was so depressed. I can only imagine how hard it was for him to spiritually feel my pain. Every time he prayed, I would feel my spirit become lighter and lighter. God was really working in me. I could feel it. His wife, co-pastor LaToya, would embrace me and show me so much love. Her smile alone would make me want to make it to another day. It was so big and bright. Some of the other women at the church would contact me via social media or by phone and encourage me. It seemed as if they were all so excited that I was visiting. I tried to attend every event they were having. Being around them would bring joy to me. The fellowship was like therapy for me.

Although I was attending and still receiving prayer, I was still frightened to get too close to anyone. I spoke to my spiritual mentor about this. She gave me some good words of encouragement. She spoke to be about trusting again. She told me that somewhere down the line, I had lost trust in God because of my lack of trust in man. I agreed. My lack of trust in people had begun to trickle down to my relationship with my Savior. It is one of the most embarrassing feelings ever. The One who created me and who was helping me get through each moment, I did not trust. After coming to this recognition, I begin to ask God for forgiveness and help.

I realized that I had to learn how to cope therefore, I needed some coping mechanisms. Before, I always loved to cook. I began to go through this cookbook that I took from my cousin. I found some great looking recipes. I was intrigued by some of them. I started cooking a new recipe every week. I would put my own spin to it and they would come out great! To comfort me and scratch the itch of me being alone, I would invite some friends and family over. Although, my fear of getting close to new people was still there, I attempted to open up to a few classmates by inviting them over for dinner as well. Soon, almost every other week, I was having dinner gatherings. Every holiday my family and some close friends would enjoy my recipe of the week together at my house.

My support system was much bigger than I thought. I had friends from college, family and friends from the new and old church, and professors encourage me all the time. After finding out some of what I had been through, classmates would applaud me for being so strong. Little did they know, it was a fight just to get out of bed every day! My professors would often push me and pull out of me what I knew was there but I had no energy to pull out.

I frequently prayed about my drinking habit and how I no longer wanted it to be a part of my life. At the beginning of a semester, I found out that for a project in my substance abuse class, we had to get rid of a habit or a substance for 12 weeks. I thought, "My prayers have been answered!" this was the perfect way to help me with my issue. During that time, I was able to get to the root of my drinking. I was able to heal and move on from that habit. Every day, I thank God that it did not get worse than it could have. It was another milestone accomplished for me.

Throughout all of this time, I would journal. This action helped me express myself. I would write when I was upset, when I was moved to write and then soon when I was happy. I began to start a "sticky note ministry" what I like to call it. I would put up sticky notes on my mirror, on my closet door, everywhere just to remind myself of some great things but mainly to encourage **MYSELF!** Some of the notes read, *"You are pretty, say it!" "No one has the right to take your happiness, so why give it to them?!" "I choose to live and not die!"* It took a while for me to really start believing what I was writing. However, every day I woke up and looked in the mirror, I would see those sticky notes and read them. Soon, my mirror became flooded with them. When my friends would come to visit me, they would be shocked to find so many. I'm sure they often thought I was a little bit loony, but they did not say. Well, at least not to me directly.

I began to talk to myself on the regular. I encouraged myself. I would tell myself, *"you WILL make it,"* every day. I would force myself up when I would feel down. When I felt myself feeling sorry for myself, I would talk to myself. I would begin to repeat the words that my pastors would pray when they prayed for me. I would repeat the words of my professors that told me I was going to make it through that class. I would call my close friends and tell them that I was feeling down and I needed a pick-me-up. I have a close friend who is like a brother to me. His name is Keith and he is a minister. I could always call on Keith and his wife. He would always call to encourage me and pray with me on the phone. Although there were many times I did not want to talk to him, let alone pray, he never gave up on me. No matter how much I had to suffer through the pain, I was going to get through it. I literally had to fight through it. I vowed that as long as I had breath in my body, I would not allow anyone or anything to take me out! It may have knocked me down, but it would not take me out.

I started noticing myself smile when someone complimented me. I began to speak more in class. I even started going out of the house more. My journal started becoming full of happy notes and thoughts. I started appreciating life and I wanted to see myself in the mirror more. I began to start wearing cute dresses and taking interest in how I presented myself again. I began to pick up my fashion styles. For one reason, the new church I attended is heavy in that area. I had to step my game up. For the second reason, I wanted my appearance to start matching my feelings. I felt new. I felt fresh and restored.

When I would think of where I was, it was like being in a dark tunnel. There was no life. No light. No hope. There was only hurt, sadness and pain. This tunnel was so dark, I could see no future. I could see no light BUT I knew there was one there somewhere. I knew it was hiding behind a wall or something. I would spend days begging for it to come out. After walking in darkness for so long, I soon came up to a spot when I wanted to give up but I looked up and saw this tiny spot that seemed like a firefly. I squinted my eyes and walked towards it. Being that I was in the dark, I stumbled on some things to get to this small dot of inspiration. However, I kept on moving. The closer I got, the larger that spot grew. Ultimately, that spot grew into the light I always knew was there. This is what I like to call: faith.

STAYING IN THE LIGHT

I stayed in college for every semester after my separation and throughout the divorce. I walked across the stage with a 3.5 GPA and an Associate in Science degree in Counseling and Human Services on May 3, 2013 from Hillsborough Community College. From 2011-2012, I served as secretary for the Brandon campus Collegiate 100 and from 2012-2013 I served as the President. I served as the 2012-2013 Vice-President of Leadership of Phi Theta Kappa National Honor Society. I received multiple certifications, awards and recognitions from Hillsborough Community College. I received letters of recommendations from the Dean of Students and many of my professors. I was often chosen to travel with the school from cities in Florida to New Orleans, LA. In October of 2013, I began the first semester of my bachelors program. Staying in school helps me stay focused. I chose to continue to stay focused so that I may accomplish my dream.

Reality of my hard work hit me when a freelance writer for a local newspaper contacted me after receiving my information from a school event. She stated that she wanted to write a story about my achievements and struggles as a single parent. It felt great being recognized for my accomplishments as well as my struggles. The article spread all over the 5 campuses of H.C.C. I was overwhelmed that people even took the time to read it, let alone congratulate me on my endeavors especially as a single mother. No one normally praise this status. However, I was grateful for that experience.

Raising both of my children alone is not an easy task. Lance is very active in my daughter's life, and I am very grateful for that. My daughter is an honor roll student. Out of the two children, the divorce affected my son most. His grades suffered the very next school year post our separation. My son can become introverted and want to be alone at times. I talk to him as much as possible about his feelings regarding the matter and he opens up as much as to be expected. After all, he is a young man. With some guidance and mentoring from our pastor, his spiritual father, his mentor, Richard and other positive male role models in his life, he is becoming better and better. I teach them the value of life. I made sure they saw me studying. I took them with me to my school events. I created chore lists for them so that they could learn responsibility. I am very pleased with them. They assist me a lot. We pray every day together. Going through the divorce was tough on them as well. We currently live in a new residence, they attend a new school and they are surrounded by new and old friends, but mainly they are surrounded by love. I do small activities with them to show them I am dedicated to being a complete mother to them. We go out for ice cream, we dance and sing together and we read and do homework together. Although it is a challenging task mothering those two, it brings me great joy to be called their mother. My ultimate goal is to show them they can overcome any adversity thrown their way. I made a vow to God that I would guide them in the direction that He wants them to go. I intend to do just that.

    I began to value my time on this earth. I spent so much time with my head hung down that I began to look up and cherish my experiences. Before, I was sort of closed minded. Once I became more open, I wanted to try new things. I tried new food, new recipes and new types of films. I wanted to see the world differently. I began to communicate differently. I wanted my speech to be different because I wanted people to notice there was a change in me. I started more coping mechanisms and stress relievers. I began to try yoga and Tai chi. I would make sure I took out personal time for myself. I would take a break for five minutes daily to do some breathing and relaxing exercises. I noticed my stress level decreasing by the day. I still would have issues with Lance, finances and other things, but it was the way I chose to respond to them. My response was different now. I valued my life. I valued my time. I appreciated myself. Therefore, I was careful with my actions. I began to care more and more about myself. I was beginning to love me!

Currently, I am happy. I am happy with myself. It had been years before I could tell anyone that. Now, I can! One of the key elements that contributed to my happiness is forgiveness. Many times, I wanted to stay angry at my situations, but I had to let anger go. As a matter of fact, I had to let a lot of things go: bitterness, hatred, regret, etc. I chose to forgive. I learned the hard way that un-forgiveness was like not brushing your teeth. When you do not brush your teeth, terrible things happen: bacteria forms and a foul odor begin to form. The foul smell begins to grow more and more and suddenly no one wants to be around you because your breath stinks. Although others are affected by your bad breath, you are the one that is harmed! This is same result for un-forgiveness. Others are affected but ultimately, you are the one that has to deal with the consequences. Therefore, I forgave. I forgave Lance, my former pastor and others. However, I mainly forgave myself. That was the best feeling of all. Now, I can be free. I can be free to love again, free to trust again and free to live again. After all, it is my choice. Now that I am content with myself, I choose life!

Lance and I speak when we have to regarding our child. We are cordial with each other. He remarried only two months after our divorce was final. Until this day, I wish him well. After some time and allowing God,

God delivered me from hatred in my heart. I am now able to freely and honestly pray for Lance and his new bride. I honestly pray that God blesses their future. My former pastor, I still care a great deal for. We are on speaking terms and I visit his church every now and then. All is forgiven. I pray all the time for his church and their increase. These are still very sore spots for me. At times, I still cry and I can still feel the pain from the scars I have. However, I am peaceful.

    I faced the fact that I was traumatized. Divorce traumatized me. I am very suspicious of new people out of fear that if I get too close to them like I used to, they will take advantage of me and harm me. God and I are still working on that one. I was afraid to date initially but rationalized dating for fun. I began dating for a short time and only for fun. I did not want anything serious out of fear of getting hurt. Although, I have gotten close to it, I have not been in a committed relationship with anyone since my divorce and I have a huge fear of remarrying, when I say huge, I mean **Huge**! Sometimes I am open to dating and other times I am not. I am, however, open to God and time healing me of all wounds. I was shown myself in a mirror throughout my divorce process and I want to be better than the woman that was looking back at me! Therefore, when or if I enter a new relationship, I can take the lessons I learned from my past experiences and apply them accordingly.

Faith is what brought me to the light. For me, it was knowing that there was a light even though I could not see one glimpse of it. Once I saw the light, I was drawn towards it. The light was my happiness. I found it eventually. When I finally found it, I grabbed on to it and vowed to not let it get as far away from me as I did before.

THE TRUTH

ABOUT MARRIAGE

In some countries, they do not get the luxury of dating and courting, but in America and with most Americans, dating and courting is expected. During this time, ground rules for how the relationship should flow should be set up. The sadness with this is, hardly anyone wants to court and date anymore. There is such a huge rush to marry with some people that they miss the joys of this experience. There used to be a time when people would say, "I wish we were like we were when we first started dating." That statement can hardly be used now because no one actually takes the time anymore to really get to know each other. This is the time where the two take the time to be intimate. Intimacy is really a word described to be vulnerable with one another, to see into one another's soul and to acknowledge the very being of that person. Marriage is only the time to enhance intimacy. The truth is intimacy should continuously be shared between the two because people are always changing. The dynamics of a relationship always change because people change. It is inevitable.

Marriage can be difficult. It is a fight. There is a fight in all of us naturally. When it is related to marriage, there is either the fight to stay married or the fight against one another. Typically, if a person wants to stay married, they fight for the marriage. In that fight includes fighting against selfishness. At times, no matter what their partner says, they stick it out. They fight through the hurt and pain but mainly they are fighting through the rejection they receive from their spouse. Once Lance had determined that he wanted to fight for the marriage, I rejected him. Most of time when people do not have an appreciation for the other person, they fight against them. This makes it more difficult for the marriage to be salvaged.

Marriage is not as easy as most people think it is. I am surprised every time I see young women stating that they can't wait to be married. They will have this type of wedding and that type of wedding. The dress will look like this and like that. This person will be invited and that person will be invited. The truth is, THEY JUST WANT THE WEDDING! They have no clue what marriage entails. Marriage is not for beauty or fame just to have the marital status read "married". It is a lifestyle. In my opinion, marriage should be in the dictionary under "hard work". Some people would beg to differ. However, it does not matter if two people are soul mates, they are meant to be together and they marry for the right reasons instead of all the wrong ones, they would still have to work hard at *staying* together.

Marriage takes communication. Speaking to each other because there is a need to, is not communication. Communication in a marriage keeps the marriage on point. It keeps everyone aware. The reason why communication is not done as much is because it causes people to be vulnerable. Being vulnerable with someone is a very sensitive feeling. It means one would have to be open. This is normally where people back down because being open is too much of a risk. The risk is typically the same with all human beings: "What if they reject me? What if they criticize me? What if they hurt me in the long run with this information? What if they judge me?" These are questions in the minds of those that are afraid to take the risk of being vulnerable. The reasons behind this action could be many. Some go back to their childhood. Others, it could be a fear to be open because of a previous relationship that went bad and they regret being open because it resulted in being hurt.

Imagine how difficult life would be without communication and not just communication from person to person. Imagine how challenging driving would be if the streets or traffic did not communicate with us. If the light did not turn red, no one would know to stop. If the sign that states "no turn on red" would not be shown, picture how many accidents would occur. A person would have to learn those signs so that they know what each sign means before driving. They must be taught how to effectively communicate. In communication there is a sender, a receiver and the message. For instance, in this driving analogy, the person is the receiver, the red light is the sender and "stop" is the message. Most times with communication the message is being sent to one party and the other party either receives it differently from what the sender intended or does not receive it at all. When this happens while we are driving, accidents occur. Damages occur. Loss of property occurs. Therefore, how can a marriage be effective if communication is lacking? This car is doomed to crash!

One of the mistakes I made in my marriage was my lack of communication. I kept a lot of things inside, to myself. I hid my hurt, embarrassment and my affair from people. I covered up my sadness like a battered woman covers up a black eye. However, it wrecked my marriage because I was too afraid of being vulnerable with my partner. In essence, I brushed it under the rug. I was afraid of what people would think of me. I had an image to uphold. I carried positions at church, work and in the community. People looked up to me. Divorce went against everything I was taught. So my beliefs were challenged. But the only thing it did was tear me down.

Communication is something that should be discussed during the courting and dating process. One will be able to determine how well a person communicates during this time. It is best to be honest and upfront with each other at all times. This will prevent any wants for hiding information from one another in the future. It will eliminate deceit and hurt towards one another. Communication does not have to be difficult. All it takes is a little trust and a risk taker.

In marriage there is sacrifice and tons of it. No one truly understands to what level of degree sacrifice is required until they are actually in the marriage. When those vows began to stare you in the face like: "for better or worse", you then began to make the choice to either sacrifice or not. In our society today, it appears no one is ready for the type of sacrifice that is required for marriage. Sacrifice requires for you to give up oneself for another. That's huge! That literally means to set your own personal wants and needs to the side for the other person. Sacrifice is when you want to stay out late with your friends when you should be home with your family. Sacrifice is continuing to sleep in the same bed with a person who has continued to hurt you. Sacrifice is nursing your sick spouse back to health when you are in the middle of disputing. Sacrifice is moving to another city away from your own family to support your spouse's dreams and goals. Sacrifice is doing what it takes to get in the sexual mood when your partner wants to make love and you do not. Sacrifice is calling to tell that person you care and will always be there even when you don't feel they deserve you. Sacrifice is a huge weight that makes up the mass to marriage. It requires the action because of the vow that was made and the love that is carried from one to another. Love is a powerful source. It can be described as a feeling, an emotion. Some people feel that it is just a simple, silly four-letter word.

Everyone loves different. Everyone shows love differently. There may be miscommunication in the way most communicates love to one another. In marriage, or any relationship for that matter, love is required. Love gives. That is why it is considered a sacrifice. We are all supposed to be loving creatures, but do we all love the way we should? Not all the time. Some of us do not even love ourselves. That is why it is hard to love others. Many times it is because we do not know the meaning of true love according to the bible. We get love confused with lust. But a marriage cannot survive on lust dear ones. There are many levels to love. It is a beautiful action that our society takes for granted. Love covers sins. What is more beautiful than Christ the Savior dying on the cross for the sins of the world? That is love and that is what marriage consists of.

    Before getting into marriage, it is imperative for one to be self-aware. This is a quality not many possess. To be self-aware is to simply being aware of one's own self. It is being aware of the thoughts, feelings and emotions; being conscious of one's character. This quality helps not only in preparation for a spouse but while dating. Self-awareness helps in the long run. I rationalized a lot of my actions in my marriage by saying that I did not get a chance to really find out who I was when I was younger because I married so young. Whose fault was that? Was it my parents fault? Was it my fault? Who knows? I did not take time to find out who I was when I was in adolescence. According to Eric Erikson, between the ages of 12 and 18, this is when an individual is faced with identity versus role confusion. This is normally the time where a person is trying to figure out who they are, what they want to be, who they want to be like and where in life they want to go. Often times this part of life is overlooked. It could be possibly overlooked by responsibility, or irresponsibility. A person could not take the time to really figure this part of life out because it was not of importance or other things were in focus. In my case, I had a lot of responsibility for a young lady. From the age of 12 to 15 I took care of my ailing grandmother. I cooked, cleaned, prepared and administered her medicine and did laundry all while trying to be a teenager, go to school and do homework. From the age of 15 to 18 I moved in with my mother and step-father and there I had the responsibility of helping out with my sisters. Although the load was not as heavy, I still helped cook and clean. I even worked a part time job. Therefore, when I was in the age section of Eric Erickson's stages of development that is called "Adolescence", I was not focusing on my identity. I did not have time to really invest in thinking about who I wanted to be. Sure, I had an idea of whom and what I wanted to do but there was no real time invested because as stated, my life was very full with responsibility. By the time I was 18, as I mentioned, I birthed my first child. There was no time invested for ValTrenda to figure out ValTrenda.

    We make critical life decisions without even knowing who we are. This is typical for most people. We think we have our life planned out according to how our parents, society and religion says we should have it and we know nothing about the core of our very being. This hurts us and others in the long run. How can we say we are ready to be married, essentially take care of another person and we do not even know who we are as a person? How is it possible to say we want to spend all of this time getting to know someone and we have not spent time alone to know who we are as an individual? How can we say that we want to love someone for the rest of our lives and not even love ourselves first? How is this possible? This is one of the reasons why marriages end up in divorce. It should be added to what society says. Society says there are three main reasons why marriages end up in divorce: finances, communication and sex. But when it is all said and done, none of those things can even take place without self. Marriage will be an easier process if one is aware of self-awareness.

Habitually we base our decisions off of society; what society says we should have by the time we are this age and such. Or, we base them off of our spiritual leaders or who we see as icons, "Well, pastor/bishop/pope says that we are to do this and that, and that's what I'm going to do." Or....we base it off of what our parents say or did, "Well, my mom was this and that and daddy says to do this and I do not care what others say, I'm going to listen to them". In order to know what decisions we should do, we must communicate to God and we do that through prayer. We must also allow Him to communicate back to us, through his word. It doesn't matter what others say or think about whom you want to pursue, or who you want to marry, it is your decision.

Marriage is beautiful and the vow should be taken very seriously. Any marriage can be fixed. Along with a lot of other elements, it takes determination, love and commitment. If you are married and you feel like giving up on your marriage, consult God about direction. No one is to judge your decision. It is ultimately between you and God. He is the one and only Judge. Many people, especially religious people argue about what the biblical law is regarding divorce. That is not *my* job. That is not *my* goal. If we spent more time addressing real issues like people marrying too young, not knowing their own identity and marrying out of lust and not love, and we spent less time arguing and bickering back and forth, maybe the divorce rate will decrease. Maybe we do marry out of love. The question is, is it real love? Real love can only come from within. You must love yourself first. Younger people see love and how much they want to be with someone because that is all they have been exposed to. What is lacking is experience. You can tell a child all day to stop running in the hallway. They will keep doing it majority of the time because all they see is what they want, until they fall. Then, they will say, "I better stop running". Maybe we, as a society, can start by educating our youth about self-awareness and teaching them by example the true meaning of love. Let's tell the truth about marriage and divorce. The issues are real but our God is bigger than our issues. He can heal any marriage. He can mend any divorced broken heart. He will forgive because He is love. And that, my friends, is the truth!

THE TRUTH ABOUT DIVORCE

It sucks! Divorce is not something I would wish on my worst enemy. Divorce leaves behind residue of unwanted feelings, hurt and pain. It is a painful process no matter how much you despise your spouse. I always tell people when you are married, it is like two hands being clasped together. The longer the marriage, the tighter the clasped becomes. In an attempt to break up or separate, that clasp that was so tight has to now rip apart. The bank accounts that were shared, the children, the property and etc., everything is now being ripped apart. When something is torn or ripped, it is not an easy feeling. Pain is usually involved. Suffering is involved. Overcoming this is indeed a process.

There are many feelings that arise during a divorce process that you may not have thought existed. Going through a divorce is like a death that took place. In actuality, a death did take place. It is the death of a relationship. Anytime a person loses someone to death, there is grief. Divorce experiences the same grief steps. Elisabeth Kübler-Ross created the **"Five Steps of Grief"** in her 1969 book *"On Death and Dying"*. The five steps are: Denial and Isolation, Anger, Bargaining, Depression and

Acceptance. There are some arguments that during breakups, people experience two additional stages: Shock and Disbelief and Guilt. During the divorce process, one may not experience all five of them and they may not all be in order. However, the average person experience more than one.

Shock and Disbelief: "I cannot believe this is happening to me!" Any one of the spouses could experience this stage. Sometimes, it may not register that the divorce is happening. This will cause a person to still go on as if they are still married to their spouse. It may seem as if they are ignoring what is going on and is totally oblivious to it.

Denial and Isolation: "It's not real, It's not happening! I just want to be alone!" When thoughts of reality begin to take place, they may be discarded by denial. This is a defense mechanism. It's an attempt to convince the brain that what is happening is not real. During the process, one may also feel alone and wants to be alone. They do not want to be comforted, they do not want to be yelled at or talked down to. They just want to feel that they have some control over the situation.

Anger: "I am mad, I can't even think straight!" During this time of the process, everything upsets the person. Anger is an outward and sometimes violent expression of hurt and feelings of lack of control.

Guilt: "This is only happening because of what I did". Many times people blame themselves for the process happening because of something they previously did or said.

Bargaining: "God, if you send my spouse back to me, I promise I will not cheat again". This is when a spouse tries to make a deal either with God or their spouse. This is a sign of lack of acceptance.

Depression: "I don't want to go on. I just want to die". Loss will most of the time bring feelings of sadness. Most times, the sadness grows and becomes so intense that it can cause a person to slip into a depressive state. This happens when a person sees that it is reality.

Acceptance: "What's done is done. I need to move on now". Once a person comes to terms with what is going on, they can accept reality. They may not agree with it, but they will accept it.

People will attempt to degrade your feelings out of ignorance. Some people mean no harm. Others are just mean, let's face it! They just see it from their own vantage point which will most times have a lot of tradition and their own personal experiences involved. People hurt us, anger us and disappoint us. But it's up to us whether we choose to stay there or chose otherwise. We can't control the situation but we have the power to control our choice. Often times we depend on others to be our back bone and our protector. We depend on others for support: emotionally, physically or financially. We expect others to be there.

Now, granted we are human and we need that human touch. We need to hear the sound of another human's voice. However, this is all for validation purposes. It's to sooth our very own insecurities. We are stronger than we think! The fight must come from within you. The fight may very well be against your own will, however, push through the pain and the hurt so that you can come out victorious. As I said, and hopefully you grasped throughout your reading, this process will be difficult. Honesty is always helpful. Be honest about your feelings. If you are angry, admit it. This will help you grow. Admitting your hurt, pain or whatever your feelings are, will help you accept what is real.

Remember, a process is an ongoing procedure. Something has to be happening for it to be considered a process. Otherwise, you are just stagnant. The longer any living object stays stagnant, the closer it becomes to death. For example, if you leave a banana out on the counter for too long, it will rot. Here's the thing about bananas, the bruising on the outside is very visual. Consequently, not only can you begin to feel like you are wasting away, but others will know you are. That includes children, family, friends, coworkers, classmates, etc.

There is absolutely nothing wrong with expressing how we feel: happiness, anger, joy, etc. But just remember that YOU control those feelings and screw what everyone says and/or thinks. There is no such thing as "She/He made me feel…" Our feelings are of our own. There are times when people may provoke certain feelings out of us, but ultimately, we own our responses. People who get off on making other people lives miserable or hurting others are only looking for some type of happiness within themselves. Try not to entertain their problem. Allow them to deal with their problem on their own. The process may get ugly, but remember your response is a reflection of your character. Just because you are legally divorced from them does not mean you have to legally hate them. Yes, you may have been deceived or you may have been the deceiver, but know that we have a choice. We must remember that trust is a choice. Trust is typically an issue for anyone coming out of a relationship not just a divorce. Moving forward may be difficult. We should stop blaming others for why we don't trust. Although others may be the reason for why it's difficult to trust, we are in control of our OWN selves! Try turning the motivation of hate into ammunition to succeed.

Divorce may leave you with bitterness. The important lesson I learned from bitterness is that it causes resentment. You will find yourself wishing negative things upon your ex. You will wish death upon them and hope that nothing good comes from their life. Before you know it, your heart is filled with this ugly disease. Often times this is a result of being heart broken. Here you are giving your life up for a person who has mistreated you and now you want revenge. You think revenge is wishing harm upon them when it is only backfiring on you. Imagine the image of a broken heart: A big red heart with that little zigzag crack down the middle. Anytime there is a crack, there is a space for something to creep inside. This is what happens to broken hearted people. Bitterness creeps in. Revenge creeps in. Vindictiveness creeps in. These things then begin to sink deeper and deeper into this crack and now become a part of the person's heart. Now, what once was consumed with love is now consumed with hate. What once was consumed with warmth is now consumed with coldness. What once was consumed with trust is now consumed with fear. Healing has to take place. You must dig deep within yourself and allow time, counsel and God to remove this disease.

Placing a bandage on a broken heart is not recommended. This happens when people move too fast. For example: jumping into another serious relationship to cover up the issue at hand. What sense would it make to place a bandage on an open wound? Imagine if a person had a piece of glass cut them down to the bone. What would happen if they went to the hospital and the doctor told them to put a bandage on it and take an over the counter pain pill? Are you kidding me?! No way! The doctor will assess them, clean out the wound and stitch it back up. Depending on the significance of the wound, surgery may have to take place. In this case, open heart surgery will need to take place. This surgery may be counseling, prayer and individual time with God or your higher power, self-care, group therapy or a combination of all of the above.

Divorce may leave you with a scar. Once you come out of surgery the doctor gives you a couple of prescriptions, a few bandages and a bill. However, one thing you are left with once surgery is complete is a scar. One thing about scars; you can always remember how you got them and how much pain it caused, but the good thing is that you learned from it, you are cautious and try to prevent it from happening again. Stay away from those who never learn from their mistakes or can never admit their wrongs. This is a sign of immaturity and lack of growth! Learn from your hurt. Allow it to show you that you are human and these things happen. Take time to heal. The longer we avoid dealing with the issue, the longer the process of healing will be. Acknowledge your strengths. It takes a very strong person to concur this. Some do not achieve it. They give up hope. So, be proud of yourself! Encourage yourself. Most importantly, chose to trust again, chose to love again and chose to live! Live happy!

NOTES & STUFF!

Made in the USA
Charleston, SC
04 May 2014